"A brilliant book. The past tw                                                   :sonally,
and I know I'm not alone. Sɔ                                          ∟ers find
refreshment and renewal in the midst of this weary world. Pastor John points
us to the rest beneath all other forms of rest: the spiritual refreshment we find
in the grace of Jesus. I highly recommend it for everyone, especially for the
weary—and double-especially for the weary who are about to go on vacation!"

**TONY MERIDA**, Pastor, Imago Dei Church, Raleigh, NC; Author, *Love Your Church*

"In these short devotions, John Hindley reminds us that rest and vacations
are good, that God gave us this world to enjoy, and that there is value
in thinking deeply about the world that God has made. It doesn't matter
whether you find rest in exploring the city or relaxing on the beach—there
is something for everyone in this book."

**COURTNEY REISSIG**, Author, *Teach Me to Feel*

"Too often our holidays are times of spiritual atrophy. We rest our bodies
but not our souls. In these little devotionals, John Hindley points us to the
glory of God in the creation around us to lift our gaze to Jesus, who gives
the deepest and sweetest rest. Read and be properly refreshed!"

**MICHAEL REEVES**, President, Union School of Theology

"As a mom of young children, getting away to 'rest' sometimes feels point-
less. I stopped packing books to read on 'vacation' a long time ago, but this
is one I won't be leaving without. It is sure to transform your family's experience of time away. Hindley's thoughtful biblical reflections beckon you to
enjoy the rest Christ offers to his own, and his engaging bits for families
make it easy to invite your children to join you."

**ABBEY WEDGEWORTH**, Author, *Held*

"This book is a rich gift! As I read, it became to me a counselor and friend. Its
format, creativity, depth, and brevity lend to its purpose: aiding Christians in
being deeply refreshed. It will serve as a guide for the individual, couple, or
family—making holidays truly times of renewal and refreshment!"

**DAVID PINCKNEY**, Rural Strategist and Northeast Regional Director, Acts 29 US

"I LOVE this book. It's refreshing, inclusive, and encouraging! A brilliant
book to take on holiday, filled with great suggestions of conversations to
have and activities to try that encourage great faith conversations with kids.
Pack it on your next family holiday!"

**AMY SMITH**, Writer, Faith in Kids

"John writes like the true pastor he is. He cuts to the issues of my sin when it comes to rest and time off—but, at the same time, I have never felt more loved or encouraged. Most of all, this book has been used to draw me closer to Christ and his heart for me. I have come away ready for the next season, no matter what it brings."

**MARK GLENN**, Pastor, The Fields Church, Southern Highlands, Australia

"*Refreshed* brings together John's pastoral heart and understanding of people's lives and struggles; his wisdom and skill in teaching and applying the breadth and depth of God's word; and his keen eye for the beauty and richness of God's creation. The result is a beautifully written book that is highly readable but also profoundly wise, rooted both in human experience and in the gospel. A great holiday companion—and a book that I'll want to come back to throughout the year."

**ANNABELLE COOMBS**, Pastoral Coordinator, St Paul's Banbury, UK

"Lots of us struggle to maintain our devotional lives on holiday. This book could help! Well-chosen Bible passages and comments work well together. The sections for families make it especially attractive for those with children."

**JULIAN HARDYMAN**, Pastor, Eden Baptist Church, Cambridge, UK

"I'm so glad someone has written this book! It's a wholehearted exhortation to enjoy all that is good in our earthly rest, while at the same time to savour the heavenly reality to which it all points. John helpfully articulates the roller coaster of emotions as expectations are fulfilled or dashed on holiday. The questions for individuals and families at the end of each study are creative, sometimes hilarious, and brilliantly imagined—helping us cultivate great habits in our family chatter, even when the holiday is over. This book will definitely be accompanying us on many holidays to come!"

**BEV DUBBERLEY**, Outreach Lead, Surrey Chapel, Norwich, UK

"This book is delightfully refreshing! John writes so simply and clearly to draw our hearts to Christ. We love how every chapter ends with fun activities and family worship. The trouble is, we now want to go on more holidays. Come, Lord Jesus!"

**TOM HART**, Arable Farmer, Suffolk, UK

# REFRESHED

## John Hindley

Refreshed (US Edition)
© John Hindley 2022

Published by:
The Good Book Company

thegoodbook.com | thegoodbook.co.uk
thegoodbook.com.au | thegoodbook.co.nz | thegoodbook.co.in

ISBN: 9781784987145 | Printed in the UK

Design by Drew McCall

*To my parents*

*Writing this book gave me the chance to revisit so many happy memories of family vacations. Splashing in the waves in Guernsey, barbecues and fries in France, and magnificent sandcastles on every beach. You gave Charles and me wonderful vacations and set a love for the sea, sun, and sand in my heart, preparing it to delight all the more in their Creator.*

# CONTENTS

# INTRODUCTION

Refreshed. Restored. Revitalized. Renewed. That's what we hope for when we go away. A break from routine, a chance for refreshment and rest, an opportunity to get some space and peace—just the thought of it is delightful. Perhaps, when we come back from our time away, we'll finally feel something like this:

> *That person is like a tree planted by streams of water,*
> *which yields its fruit in season*
> *and whose leaf does not wither—*
> *whatever they do prospers.*     *(Psalm 1:3)*

You can probably imagine the scene. A sunny meadow where the clear waters of a river supply life to a lush and abundant tree, laden with fruit. This tree stands strong and tall even when storms come. Quenched with deep draughts of life, it provides sweetness and joy to all around.

Some trips away linger in the memory with sun-soaked beauty—they genuinely refresh us, giving us a glimpse of what it's like to be that well-watered tree. But it's not always that way. Things go wrong, people get ill, family members are fractious, or the weather turns sour. Some trips just make us wish we were back home!

There's one kind of refreshment we can always count

on, though. The person in Psalm 1 isn't someone who's just come back from a great trip. It's someone "whose delight is in the law of the Lord, and who meditates on his law day and night" (v 2). The "law of the Lord" means the Scriptures. The Bible is a book written by the Holy Spirit, at the pleasure of God, our Father, to refresh us, strengthen us, establish us and make us fruitful by showing us Jesus, his Son.

Trips away from home allow us time, space and the inclination to look, to ponder and to wonder again at God. They give us the opportunity to rest in the Lord's goodness and glory. We go away to be refreshed, and the Lord also wants to give us spiritual refreshment. He invites us to spend our vacation with him: to know true rest, to let our roots grow deeper into the one who offers us living water (John 4:10), and to become those from whom that same refreshment flows out to others (John 7:37-39).

This book is designed to help you enjoy our Lord Jesus, in his Bible and in the world he created, while you are away. Just as we often turn to a devotional book for Advent or Lent, marking those seasons when life feels different with appropriate Bible readings, so times away lend themselves to the same approach. I want to invite you to fully enjoy the season of rest you're in. Maybe you're planning to relax by the pool, hit the city streets, or hike up as many mountains as possible. Maybe you'll travel alone, with friends or relatives, or with small children in tow. Whichever, the chapters in this book have been written for you—to help you soak in the Scriptures, so that everything you see and do starts to draw your heart to the God who made it all.

## HOW TO USE THIS BOOK

This book is made up of 30 devotional Bible studies— each one with a Bible passage to read, a short reflection on the passage, and an idea to help you keep your mind on Christ throughout the day. They're divided into sections depending on what sort of place or theme they fit. Some relate to the type of place you might be visiting. Others address wider themes common to many trips. This means that you can use the book in whatever way best fits you. I'd suggest that you start with the "arriving" or "rest" chapters and then pick others according to what you are doing each day. If you're on a really long trip, you could even read it all from beginning to end!

Each of the daily reflections is primarily written for adults, but at the end of each study there are resources to help you use it as the basis of a family Bible time. There are a couple of questions to help get a conversation going, plus a suggested activity to help you have fun and engage with God's word as a family.

However you use this book, and whatever sort of trip you are taking, my prayer for you is that you will see Jesus. And that seeing Jesus, you will be like a tree planted by streams of water: deeply refreshed.

# Arriving

*¹ I lift up my eyes to the mountains –*
*    where does my help come from?*
*² My help comes from the* LORD,
*    the Maker of heaven and earth.*

*³ He will not let your foot slip –*
*    he who watches over you will not slumber;*
*⁴ indeed, he who watches over Israel*
*    will neither slumber nor sleep.*

*⁵ The* LORD *watches over you –*
*    the* LORD *is your shade at your right hand;*
*⁶ the sun will not harm you by day,*
*    nor the moon by night.*

*⁷ The* LORD *will keep you from all harm –*
*    he will watch over your life;*
*⁸ the* LORD *will watch over your coming and going*
*    both now and forevermore.*

*Psalm 121*

# 1. HOPES AND FEARS

Psalm 121

A few weeks ago my wife and I sat with a cup of tea, newly arrived at our friends' home, enjoying the sun and grateful for a break after a tiring few months. We were lazily wondering whether this might be the trip when our girls would at last be old enough to play on their own while we both read a book. This happy thought was interrupted by our oldest daughter racing up the garden to tell us that her sister's arm was pointing the wrong way. Flick, my wife, spent the first night of our vacation in the hospital with her; then there was an operation, a cast... and a different couple of weeks to the ones we had been hoping for.

That is why Psalm 121 is a good psalm for the start of a vacation. The traveler praying this psalm lifts his eyes to the mountains. He sees the road snaking up through foothills and disappearing into the haze. He knows that the pass is high and that it will be days before he is descending into the far valley. What he does not know is what the mountains hold.

He may enjoy a walk through upland meadows, with flowers and sweet sunlight speeding his steps as he enjoys easy conversation with others he has met on the way. Or the weather may close in, bringing fog or storms, the wind lashing sleet into his eyes as he struggles to keep to the path. The voices he hears may be the shouted cries of bandits as he runs for his life.

He does not know what the mountains hold. But he knows that he is held by God. This traveler's help does not come from his own planning, wisdom, strength or speed. His help comes from the Lord—the Maker of heaven and earth. The mighty God, a great and powerful friend, is the one who keeps us from harm and guards our lives. We know the extent of his reach: he is triumphant over death, evil and all powers natural and supernatural. We know the extent of his love: he won this triumph through dying in our place on the cross.

You do not know what this time away holds. You have hopes. You may well have fears. You might read this feeling full of light and joy, or you might feel you're already at the end of yourself. Perhaps you're aware of conversations that need to be had or pressure that must be relieved. You are tired, maybe. The Lord knows; he sees; he watches over you. He is already in the mountains, and he will watch over your coming and going this week. He cares for you, and he's the one who made heaven and earth.

## FOR TODAY

Write out verses 1 and 2 (or the whole psalm) and put them in a place where you will see them as you wake up. Use them to form a prayer each morning as you lift your eyes to what the day may hold. You might like to say them out loud as you do so.

## FOR THE FAMILY

### Ask

- What are you hoping for over this time away? Are you worried about anything?
- Why do you think it's a good idea to think a bit about Jesus together while we're here?

### Make

Do the activity above as a family. Everyone can write out and decorate their own verses, or you could do them on a big piece of paper together (or with stones on the beach, or something else—be creative!). As you decorate your verses, talk together about your hopes and fears for the vacation. Maybe you want to write them around the verses. You could then use them as a basis for prayer together. Then put the paper up somewhere so you can come back to it on subsequent days (or make the photo of the stones on the beach your phone wallpaper).

**She**

<sup>10</sup> *My beloved spoke and said to me,*
  *"Arise, my darling,*
    *my beautiful one, come with me.*
<sup>11</sup> *See! The winter is past;*
    *the rains are over and gone.*
<sup>12</sup> *Flowers appear on the earth;*
    *the season of singing has come,*
    *the cooing of doves*
      *is heard in our land.*
<sup>13</sup> *The fig tree forms its early fruit;*
    *the blossoming vines spread their fragrance.*
  *Arise, come, my darling;*
    *my beautiful one, come with me."*

**He**

<sup>14</sup> *My dove in the clefts of the rock,*
    *in the hiding places on the mountainside,*
  *show me your face,*
    *let me hear your voice;*
  *for your voice is sweet,*
    *and your face is lovely.*
<sup>15</sup> *Catch for us the foxes,*
    *the little foxes*
  *that ruin the vineyards,*
    *our vineyards that are in bloom.*

*Song of Songs 2:10-15*

# 2. A BRIGHT SHADOW

Song of Songs 2:10-15

Christ has given you this time as a chance to come away with him—have you thought of it that way? It's a chance to come away from your normal life, and to come to him. As such, it is a bright shadow of the day when he will return and we will see his face. In the Bible's great love song, the Song of Songs, the author, Solomon, entreats his beloved to arise and come away with him. He does so by evoking the welcome sweetness of spring after winter has passed. The beauty of the budding flowers and first ripe figs and the fragrance of the blossom impel him to seek his beloved: she is just as sweet and delightful to him.

Solomon pictures for us the love that Christ has for his bride. The bride of Christ is his people: you and me (see Ephesians 5:25-33). The difference between Jesus and Solomon is that Christ made the flowers and figs. It was he who decided that vines should not merely give fruit but should do so with beautiful blossom and heady fragrance. Jesus has filled his creation with beauty and sweetness. The simple reason is that he delights in his bride and wants to make our life delightful in turn.

This trip that you are beginning is not so much a well-earned break as a gift. Plenty of people work hard for no rest, and yet Christ has given you time to head away from the daily grind. It must be because he has some particular blessing to give you—something that you could not experience at home, in the normal rhythms of life. There will be all sorts of glimpses of his face. And there is a thought that can unite these moments of bliss, making each even more glorious. It is that Jesus has brought you out of normal life now in order to foreshadow the day when he will come and do that ultimately and eternally.

One of the joys of time away is a break from regular stresses, whether at home or work. With more space, more time and (hopefully) more sun, we hope for deep rest, joy, peace and laughter. We appreciate things that we don't have time to notice during a busy week at work. A new place gives us new perspectives.

We arrive with high expectations, often—but with a sense of sadness too. We know this break will be short-lived. Maybe you had a vacation last year, and the peace seemed to evaporate after only a few days back home. If so, then here is a thought to ponder. This day you are in now, this holy-day, is closer to real life, in some ways, than most days of the year—because it points to the deepest reality. In its peace and wonder, its rest and joy, today hints at the day of Christ's return. After all, Jesus has given us the promise that he is coming back for his bride. We will "come away" and live with him, day after day, in unending joy and wonder. This trip is not a temporary evasion of reality but a reminder that much of what passes for reality is as fleeting as the mist on a summer's morning. The true reality is Jesus, and he is wooing us to come away with him to sweet-scented vineyards of everlasting love.

## FOR TODAY

See if you can find a spot, a vista, a song on your phone, a sweet-smelling flower or some other beauty that lifts your heart. Take a minute or two to focus on it as you give thanks to Christ for his love and for the future he has prepared for you. Maybe ask for grace to enjoy this break away for what it is—a bright shadow of that future glory.

## FOR THE FAMILY

### Ask

- What have you seen or done so far that you have really enjoyed or appreciated?
- How can you enjoy this even more by seeing it as a gift from Jesus?

### Chat

Take some time over a meal or in the car—any time when it's easy to chat together—to ask what you all love about the place you are vacationing in already. What have you done or seen or smelt or tasted that you want every day while you are here? Then talk about the new creation, the world we will live in when Jesus returns and everything is made good and perfect again. We do not know details, but what might it be like?

I asked this once and was told with certainty that we would ride on flying unicorns. I hope so.

# Rest

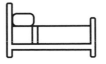

*[Jesus said,]* [27] *"All things have been committed to me by my Father. No one knows the Son except the Father, and no one knows the Father except the Son and those to whom the Son chooses to reveal him.*

[28] *"Come to me, all you who are weary and burdened, and I will give you rest.* [29] *Take my yoke upon you and learn from me, for I am gentle and humble in heart, and you will find rest for your souls.* [30] *For my yoke is easy and my burden is light."*

*Matthew 11:27-30*

# 3. WEARY AND HEAVY LADEN

## Matthew 11:27-30

We come away to rest. This looks different depending on our personality. I remember the enthusiasm of a friend telling me about how many mountains he was planning to climb one summer. I felt tired just listening, as I dreamed instead of long afternoons spent reading on a sun lounger! There's one thing my friend and I have in common, though: we crave rest. It's the same for all of us. We get tired of our work responsibilities, home projects and ministry roles. The idea of letting go and having just a week or two away from the office and from church can feel like pure freedom.

When we feel weary and heavy laden, we sometimes start to nurse resentment toward those who burden us. They may be in the wrong—an over-demanding boss, perhaps. But often they are not. Family, friends and brothers and sisters in Christ rightly take up our time and energy. Yet we resent them because we are so tired!

Perhaps it is God himself you resent. After all, he has allowed your life to become this crowded. His people have helped put the burdens onto your back. You have little hope that God will grant you the rest you need, so you decide you must grasp it for yourself. There are times when, leaving home for a rest, I have shut my Bible as firmly as my laptop. This is as foolish as it is wrong! The wonderful truth is that Jesus sees our burdens.

Jesus sees what you carry and he says, "Come to me, all you who are weary and burdened, and I will give you rest." He knows you carry burdens, and he does not dismiss or diminish them. Actually, he takes them more seriously than you do yourself. He knows that laying them down for just a few days is not enough. He knows that shifting them onto your partner or friends will not really get rid of them. Jesus sees what you carry, and he offers to bear it with you—*for* you. He urges you to be yoked to him: to come into partnership with the God who made you. He offers to take your burdens and give you rest.

Maybe that feels impossible. Our burdens can be so many, so complex, so weighty. But notice that Christ addresses "little children" (v 25). He is not talking only to infants—he's putting all of us, whatever our age, into that group. I remember as a young child being overwhelmed by math homework. It seemed an insurmountable task. Then my mother helped me, sitting by my side and guiding me through. To the God of infinite wisdom, complete patience and endless kindness, our burdens are as simple as those basic sums.

Come to the one who can give you rest. Come, whether you run or crawl. Jesus sees your burdens; he knows you are weary and weak. He promises, "I will give you rest."

## FOR TODAY

If you feel heavy laden, take five minutes to write a list of your burdens. Or you might just like to ponder them, or draw a picture of yourself weighed down by them. Then remind yourself that Jesus sees these, agrees that you are weary with bearing them and offers you rest. Do not seek to lose or lighten the load. Instead, come to Jesus in prayer; thank him for seeing you and ask him to give you rest. There may be more to do later—time away can provide space and distance to reassess our workload and rhythms. But for now, simply ask your Lord for rest in the knowledge that he has promised to carry your burdens.

## FOR THE FAMILY

### Ask

- Is there anything back at home that has been making you worried or tired or making life feel hard?
- Jesus says that he will give us rest. What do you think rest looks and feels like? How does Jesus help us to experience this?

### Chat

Talk about what you brought with you. What did you bring, and what did you leave? Is there anything you wish you'd brought or you wish you hadn't brought? What about the things you enjoy and the things you worry about at home—what is here, and what is left behind?

What about Jesus—is God here or did he stay at home? How could you give your burdens to him now?

<sup>1</sup> *God is our refuge and strength,*
    *an ever-present help in trouble.*
<sup>2</sup> *Therefore we will not fear, though the earth give way*
    *and the mountains fall into the heart of the sea,*
<sup>3</sup> *though its waters roar and foam*
    *and the mountains quake with their surging.*

<sup>4</sup> *There is a river whose streams make glad the city of God,*
    *the holy place where the Most High dwells.*
<sup>5</sup> *God is within her, she will not fall;*
    *God will help her at break of day.*
<sup>6</sup> *Nations are in uproar, kingdoms fall;*
    *he lifts his voice, the earth melts.*

<sup>7</sup> *The* Lord *Almighty is with us;*
    *the God of Jacob is our fortress.*

<sup>8</sup> *Come and see what the* Lord *has done,*
    *the desolations he has brought on the earth.*
<sup>9</sup> *He makes wars cease*
    *to the ends of the earth.*
 *He breaks the bow and shatters the spear;*
    *he burns the shields with fire.*
<sup>10</sup> *He says, "Be still, and know that I am God;*
    *I will be exalted among the nations,*
    *I will be exalted in the earth."*

<sup>11</sup> *The* Lord *Almighty is with us;*
    *the God of Jacob is our fortress.*

                                        *Psalm 46*

# 4. STOPPING

Psalm 46

I struggle to stop. I feel anxious about things I should be doing, even if there is nothing that I really should be doing. I even manage to make relaxing into a task that needs doing, and then that makes me feel stressed! You might be different than me—maybe you ease into rest and relaxation as naturally as a foot into a slipper. If so, this study might be an opportunity to enjoy the blessing of stopping even more deeply.

If you are more like me, this is a challenge and an invitation. A challenge because to lay aside our activity is to admit that our work, our tasks, our busyness and productivity are not central to who we are. For many of us, that's what they have become. We identify ourselves by what we do day to day.

Perhaps you studied long and hard, worked your way up or labored for late hours to hold the position you now have, and it's become who you are. The principal at our school was a figure of awe, even fear, to me as a boy. Bumping into him on a beach on vacation, in an old T-shirt and shorts as grubby as mine, was a strange experience (although I still found myself hastily tucking in my shirt). For him, I sensed it was terrible. To be seen outside his suit, study and dignified professionalism must have been hard—like a loss of identity.

Perhaps it is not the work you do but how you do it. You love being busy at home, at work, in the family. You also love having that reputation. You bask when others tell you that they don't know how you do it all. You enjoy the fact that the pastor said that he knows you are busy, but could you just... Perhaps you savor the knowing half-smiles of other busy people when you tell them you are tired. This medal of honor is understood well by fellow veterans.

The Lord takes us aside to stop. Even in a situation of extreme stress, the sons of Korah, who wrote this psalm, find their confidence in God. He is their fortress, refuge and strength. To truly know this, we need to be still. Either it is our activity that is decisive or God's. Either we save ourselves, define ourselves, create ourselves—or God does. On the day of Christ, no one will ask us for a timesheet.

This is challenging for some of us—and yet, what freedom! Freedom to stand in clear air, still and knowing that God is the one who saves us and defines us—that it was his hand that created us and his smile that will welcome us home. Our manic activity and busyness are not needed. God will be exalted among the nations, and in us. This will be his achievement and not ours. So we can breathe, be still and know that he is God.

## FOR TODAY

Find as much space and time as you can at one point today to be still. Stand looking at the view, walk slowly and aimlessly, or sit on a sofa or lounge chair. Then try to stay there! As thoughts crowd in, whisper the words of the psalm: "Be still, and know that God is God."

## FOR THE FAMILY
### Ask

- What do we like doing as a family? What activities do we all find really fun? What does it look like for us to relax and "be still" together?
- Do you think of God as a busy person, rushing around and getting lots done, or as a still person, enjoying hanging out with friends and resting?

### Spot

Watch out for the most relaxed people you can find today. Keep count: who can spot the largest number of really chilled people? And who can spot the single most chilled out person?

# Friends & Family

*⁷ So Moses went out to meet his father-in-law [Jethro] and bowed down and kissed him. They greeted each other and then went into the tent. ⁸ Moses told his father-in-law about everything the LORD had done to Pharaoh and the Egyptians for Israel's sake and about all the hardships they had met along the way and how the LORD had saved them.*

*⁹ Jethro was delighted to hear about all the good things the LORD had done for Israel in rescuing them from the hand of the Egyptians. ¹⁰ He said, "Praise be to the LORD, who rescued you from the hand of the Egyptians and of Pharaoh, and who rescued the people from the hand of the Egyptians. ¹¹ Now I know that the LORD is greater than all other gods, for he did this to those who had treated Israel arrogantly."*

*Exodus 18:7-11*

# 5. VISITING

Exodus 18:7-11

Moses was a mere shepherd when he last saw Jethro, his father-in-law. Now, he is the mighty prophet God has chosen to lead Israel out of slavery in Egypt. He has called down God's judgment on a wicked king; he has parted a sea. Moses is still a humble man, and approaches Jethro with due respect and love. But how will Jethro respond to Moses' appointment as prophet of the Lord? What will this time together bring?

Families are strange, with complicated relationships. Friendships can be just as hard to navigate, especially if one friend has suffered or life has changed. Who are you visiting? What are the hopes you cherish and the fears you nurse? Such visits can be free and joyful. Or a reluctant duty. Most often they lie somewhere in the middle. You are looking forward to seeing your friend, but will it be different after his wedding? You parted with your sister on good terms last time, but what about those unresolved issues under the surface? You feel sick as you drive, not only because this might be the last time you see her but because she still has not accepted Christ as her Savior.

It's likely Moses is unsure, conflicted, both hopeful and fearful as he kisses Jethro. He then takes his courage in his hand and tells Jethro everything the Lord has done.

His speech is full of God's mighty work and kind salvation. The response should fill us with hope. Jethro is delighted and transformed, declaring, "Now I know that the LORD is greater than all other gods."

Maybe your response is like mine: to smile wryly and think, *That's good for Moses, but it's not always so simple.* You are right. Families and friendships are complicated and deep. There are matters that have their roots in things that happened years, even generations, ago. Yet you do not travel alone. The Spirit of God, who was with Moses, is in you. The same mighty power that blew the sea apart and gave Moses grace to speak the truth to Jethro is at work in you.

Who knows how things will go when you sit down to dinner? Who knows if there will be the same competitiveness as when you were young? Who knows if you can forgive or will be forgiven? Who knows if there is any chance of hearing fairly or of being heard? Who knows what the others are fearing, brooding on, hoping and carrying? This we do know, though: Christ will be at the table with you. He is there with forgiveness and forbearance, grace and truth. He comes with power to redeem the sins of generations and increase the joy of reunions. He gave you to your family and friends, and he gave them to you, and his purpose in all of this is life and not death.

## FOR TODAY

Can you open up your hopes and fears before the Lord, and before those you are traveling with? It's tempting to rehearse conversations in your head, whether with delight or with terror. Instead, try rehearsing what the Lord has done for you. Call to mind how deeply he loves you and how deeply he loves those you are visiting. You are loved and welcomed into the family of our Father, so go with hope and peace—you do not go alone.

## FOR THE FAMILY

### Ask

- What are you looking forward to about this visit? Is there anything you are worried about?
- How did God use the time Moses had with Jethro to encourage them both? How might he use our visit to encourage us and those we're visiting?

### Do

Get out a family album or open your photo app and talk about who you are going to see. Remember good times with them (we don't take photos of the arguments!) and then also gently ask if there have been any times that were harder. How can you pray for each other as you go to see family or friends? How can you pray for them? How can you work as a team to bless them and each other?

*5:21 Submit to one another out of reverence for Christ.
22 Wives, submit yourselves to your own husbands as you
do to the Lord. ...*

*25 Husbands, love your wives, just as Christ loved the
church and gave himself up for her 26 to make her
holy, cleansing her by the washing with water through
the word, 27 and to present her to himself as a radiant
church, without stain or wrinkle or any other blemish,
but holy and blameless. ...*

*6:1 Children, obey your parents in the Lord, for this is
right. 2 "Honor your father and mother" – which is the
first commandment with a promise – 3 "so that it may
go well with you and that you may enjoy long life on the
earth."*

*4 Fathers, do not exasperate your children; instead, bring
them up in the training and instruction of the Lord.*

*Ephesians 5:21-22, 25-27; 6:1-4*

# 6. TENSIONS

Ephesians 5:21-22, 25-27; 6:1-4

As a child I used to whine, "Are we there yet?" right as we pulled away from our home. My dad particularly appreciated that! Trips away often provide more time together with spouses and children. Sometimes things flow smoothly—everyone is kind and happy and appreciative, and everything is a delight. Those are the breaks advertised by travel agencies! But the ads don't show us the arguments, the hurts and the times when you just wish you were back at home. Sadly, times away together can be the final moment in a marriage or a confirmation of distance between parents and children, siblings or friends.

A lot of the time it is a mix. There are often enough good times to make a highlights video or album from the photos. But there are also days when nobody takes the camera out. You might long for a family to travel with, or the family you travel with might leave you feeling out of place—unknown, unseen and unheard.

If the cracks that have been revealed by your time away are deep and long-established, what you need now is probably to simply turn to prayer. The trip will not have caused these divisions and pain and is unlikely to heal them. The Lord can and will work in them, though. Turning to him now, and then seeking some wise counsel on your return, may be the best thing.

But it may be that the tensions spring from no more than the strangeness of a different routine. Perhaps you are all just being catty with each other, picking on and griping at one another—there's no obvious reason except that you are all sinners. In this case, it might not be worth searching too hard for the causes of the arguments. Better to reach for something that will certainly help. We can transform everything by simple submission.

A few years ago, the Lord struck me with the realization that vacations were not my well-earned right to self-indulgence but an opportunity to serve my wife and children. I have not applied this consistently, but repenting in this area has allowed me to see them flourish when we are away (and has given me far better vacations). When my wife and I both live this way, it is truly delightful. Even when only one of us manages to be selfless, both are blessed.

The verse to memorize, write out or meditate on is the first one above: Ephesians 5:21. Then, if you like, look up the whole passage and read the section that most applies to you as a wife, husband, child or parent. This break from routine is not a break from godliness, where you get to be selfish! And that is good news. There is no joy for you in selfishness, and none for your family either. You need the Holy Spirit's work in you, so you need to pray, and then simply watch and notice those you are with. How can you empathize, how can you enter in, how can you bless them?

## FOR TODAY

Pray that you would notice those you are with. Then look for opportunities to give them the rest they long for. Maybe it'll be doing the washing-up or playing a game with your children or running your spouse a really nice bath. This time tomorrow, look back and see if there was greater joy in your heart and your family.

## FOR THE FAMILY
### Ask

• What causes arguments while we are away together? What do you do to contribute to them?
• Do you think you will have a better time today if the rest of the family is kind, patient and forgiving with you? Do you think you will have a better time if you are kind, forgiving and patient with the rest of us? How can we get God to help us with that?

### Spot

In my family we have sometimes found that spotting grumpiness or meanness in each other can make a good game. When it is spotted by an adult (or by anyone if you are feeling brave!), the person in question has to do 20 jumping jacks or 50 trampoline bounces (or whatever—anything that's invigorating and not too hard!). Or try making a rule that they need to leave the room and come back in to try again. It's a game that needs monitoring, but it can shift a snarky atmosphere into a comedic one.

# Skies

¹ L ORD, *our Lord,*
    *how majestic is your name in all the earth!*

*You have set your glory*
    *in the heavens.*
² *Through the praise of children and infants*
    *you have established a stronghold against your*
        *enemies,*
    *to silence the foe and the avenger.*
³ *When I consider your heavens,*
    *the work of your fingers,*
 *the moon and the stars,*
    *which you have set in place,*
⁴ *what is mankind that you are mindful of them,*
    *human beings that you care for them?*

⁵ *You have made them a little lower than the angels*
    *and crowned them with glory and honor.*
⁶ *You made them rulers over the works of your hands;*
    *you put everything under their feet:*
⁷ *all flocks and herds,*
    *and the animals of the wild,*
⁸ *the birds in the sky,*
    *and the fish in the sea,*
    *all that swim the paths of the seas.*

⁹ L ORD, *our Lord,*
    *how majestic is your name in all the earth!*

                       *Psalm 8 (A psalm of David)*

# 7. STARS

Psalm 8

I remember driving from Manchester, the city where we lived, through an icy night to visit my wife's family in rural Norfolk. As I climbed stiffly out of the car, the glory of the heavens filled my senses. On that crisp night, with no streetlights for miles, the stars blazed with majesty. It was wondrous.

Christ has set lights in the darkness. He has done so as testimony to the eternal victory of light over darkness. He has done so as a picture of his people scattered as light-bringers across a dark world. He has also done so to remind us of our place.

David was used to months spent in the wilderness, fleeing from the forces of jealous King Saul, and later on campaign when he was king himself. As he lay in the stillness, his heart was drawn to praise and his mind to poetry.

The Lord's name is majestic, and he has set the glory of his majesty in the heavens!

So often, as a busy adult, I miss this, but then my eyes are turned to the spreading glory of the skies by my children's hushed "Wow!" Thus the Lord establishes his stronghold (v 2). His enemies have many weapons to dismay and drag our hearts away from their Creator, but the Lord has far more light than his enemies have darkness—far more glory than they have misery. Just look up!

Look up and consider what sort of might and power Christ has in his words. He is the Word of God (John 1:1-3), who spoke the stars into existence in an instant. All that majesty and artistry come from Jesus' simple words. The divine Master spreads out a canvas of limitless breadth and paints with light. Who are we when compared with such a magnificent work? How could God, who has such a command of both beauty and power, be interested in a grubby little bug like me?

The answer is more amazing than the whirling galaxies. It is humanity that is crowned with glory and honor (Psalm 8:5). God did not enter his creation as a star. The light of the world came as a baby. It was humanity that he took on, humanity where the eternal light dwells. We are crowned with the glory and honor of God.

As the people of Christ the Light, we are rulers over the works of God's hands. We are lords of the stars! He has given us this place because he loves us. So the pageantry of the heavens is not the self-interested work of a conceited artist. Instead, its beauty and power are a declaration of care by a lover to his beloved. Each night Jesus tells us to open our eyes and see the sparkling lights that declare his love more deeply than any gold-set diamonds.

## FOR TODAY

If there is a clear night, take some time to look up. Sit in the quiet with a favorite drink, lie on your back on the grass or linger in the cold as you absorb some of the wonder that the heavens hold. Feel the wonder of how deeply you are loved. (If you can't see the stars, look around you at other wonderful parts of God's creation instead!)

## FOR THE FAMILY

### Ask

• When you look up at the stars at night, how do you feel? What about if you look at them and think about how Christ made them?
• How do you feel about Jesus as you look at the stars?

### Do

How can you see and remember the stars, both now and when you return home? Why not choose a night with a good forecast, stay up late with some snacks and take photos, paint pictures, or write a poem. Try to capture some of the glory of the heavens as you sit together under their beauty. Or, if the sun sets too late for your family, you could always watch a documentary or online video about the stars instead.

*[12] [Jesus said] "I am the light of the world. Whoever follows me will never walk in darkness, but will have the light of life."*

*John 8:12*

*[1] The heavens declare the glory of God;*
  *the skies proclaim the work of his hands.*
*[2] Day after day they pour forth speech;*
  *night after night they reveal knowledge.*
*[3] They have no speech, they use no words;*
  *no sound is heard from them.*
*[4] Yet their voice goes out into all the earth,*
  *their words to the ends of the world.*
 *In the heavens God has pitched a tent for the sun.*
*[5] It is like a bridegroom coming out of his chamber,*
  *like a champion rejoicing to run his course.*
*[6] It rises at one end of the heavens*
  *and makes its circuit to the other;*
  *nothing is deprived of its warmth.*

*Psalm 19:1-6 (A psalm of David)*

# 8. SUN

John 8:12; Psalm 19:1-6

The skies are there every day, but away from home we are often more conscious of them. It might be that sunshine is flickering off wave-tops or reflecting from snow to make the world gleam. Perhaps the clouds are brooding over hills, or the moon is half-hidden by wisps of morning mist. We are more aware of the heavens because we have more time, perhaps. If we are most often in a city, the absence of buildings and streetlights increases our sense of the openness of beach or wilderness.

These heavens declare the glory of God. They don't merely hint at his goodness; they "pour forth speech," unfailingly, "day after day" and with such volume that their words go "to the ends of the world." In the heavens God has given us an inescapable call to worship. This isn't a call to worship creation or a vague generic deity. The cry of the heavens is far more specific.

As David watched the skies turn from darkness to dawn, the Holy Spirit showed him the light of a bridegroom. The splendor of the sun transforms the darkness just as the love of Christ, the great Bridegroom of his people (Ephesians 5:25-27), transforms our lives.

Transfixed, David watches the rising sun as it begins its daily circuit of the heavens. There is nothing that will remain hidden from it. No coldness unwarmed, no darkness unexposed. Like a champion, a mighty warrior, it will set at the day's end undaunted and undefeated. So Christ, the great champion of our hope, warms and enlightens our world. Indeed, Jesus draws a comparison between the sun and himself when he declares that he is the light of the world (John 8:12).

Jesus is reminding us that the sun is a visual aid of his light. He is not simply making a comparison. When the great boxer Muhammad Ali claimed he would "float like a butterfly, sting like a bee," he was comparing his boxing with the agility of the butterfly's flight and the strength of the bee's sting. When Jesus said he was the light of the world, he was not doing the same. Ali did not create butterflies and bees to display his skill and strength. Jesus did create the sun to reveal his warmth and light. He made the sun so that we could know the sort of light that he is and that he gives.

Everything that the sun does in and for us is a picture of the greater light that Jesus gives us. Without the sun there is no life, no joy, no hope. But think what it feels like to stand and bask in the sun—that is a picture of Jesus' love for you. Without the sun there is no warmth, no lazy summer afternoons, no briskly bright winter walks. We have a Light who dazzles us with joy and leads us in truth. He put a shiny thing in the sky to help us remember.

## FOR TODAY

As you go through the day, try to notice the things you enjoy that rely, directly or indirectly, on the sun. Make a list if that works for you. Use this as the basis of a prayer of thanks this evening, and also to consider how all these blessings and more flow from Christ to you.

## FOR THE FAMILY
### Ask

• What do you think would happen if the sun stopped shining? What would life be like?
• Jesus made the sun to show us what he is like. He says he is the light of the world. What would life be like without him? How does he bring light and warmth into our lives?

### Do

Make a list together as in the "for today" section above. Or, for a simpler option, just stand in the sun together, bask in its warmth and enjoy the idea that Jesus' love for you is this warm and this light.

*¹⁰ The land you are entering to take over is not like the land of Egypt, from which you have come, where you planted your seed and irrigated it by foot as in a vegetable garden. ¹¹ But the land you are crossing the Jordan to take possession of is a land of mountains and valleys that drinks rain from heaven. ¹² It is a land the Lord your God cares for; the eyes of the Lord your God are continually on it from the beginning of the year to its end.*

*Deuteronomy 11:10-12*

# 9. RAIN

Moses spoke these words to Israel, the people whom God had chosen as his own, led out of slavery in Egypt and brought to the edge of their own land. Just like Eden before it, the land of Israel was meant to be a spreading gift. The people of Israel were to be a light to the other nations—they were to show and tell of the kindness, glory and majesty of God. As a picture of this, Israel was a land particularly dependent on the direct mercy of the Lord. It needed rain.

Back in Egypt, the land was watered by hard work. Moses reminded the freed slaves of how it had needed irrigating by foot—the workers tending to their meager water-channels to make the water go further. It was back-breaking work. The water originated in the Nile but the immediate means of conveying it to growing crops was the ingenuity and sweat of the people.

It was very different in the land of Israel. Here the fields, the crops, the life of God's people, depended directly on the rain. If God sent the rain, it would be a plentiful, lush and fertile land. This was a land of plenty, a land flowing with milk and honey, with sweetness as well as sustenance. As long as the rains fell.

As I write, on a dreary January day, I wish it would *stop* raining so that I can get some fresh air. Rain can be the worst forecast, especially in your precious few weeks of the year off work—heralding whole days of trying to find things to do that are slightly more interesting than scrolling endlessly on your phone! But think what it would mean for the rain to stop.

A couple of years ago I found myself on the phone with a friend who is a farmer. It had been an unusually dry winter, and he asked me to pray. He was in his tractor, sowing a crop—and he said he had left it as late as he dared. If there was no rain in the next few days, the crop would be lost. As I hung up, I reflected that we are all like that field: we are utterly dependent on the Lord for life. If our Lord did not send rain, Tom's crop would die. If he had not sent us his Spirit, his Word, his very life, then we would wither faster than any sprouting grain.

If rainfall disrupts your plans, let it become a picture of the kindness of God. How long would you survive this world—and even this brief time away—without the Holy Spirit showering you with kindness, mercy, love, forgiveness, guidance and life itself? We do not deserve the rain; we deserve to cry out, "I am thirsty." Yet it was Christ who cried this on the cross (John 19:28). He suffered the most terrible thirst so that we could be quenched by his Spirit. He died in the dryness of the wilderness so that streams of living water would flow to and from us in forgiveness and love (John 7:38).

As for Tom, our Father sent the rain, and the grain grew. God is like that.

## FOR TODAY

What has rain spoiled, cost or messed up for you during this time away? What has it given you? How can you enjoy the rain rather than resent it? If you're feeling brave, go out in it! Marvel at how it cleans away dust, rejuvenates plants and brings life to all around.

## FOR THE FAMILY
### Ask

- What do you like about the rain? What do you dislike? What would we miss out on if there were no rain?
- What could we do today (or the next rainy day) that would be really fun? How could this help us remember that God sends us kindness and love just like he sends the rain?

### Make

Make a rain catcher and a chart to measure how much rain you get each day while you are away. By a rain catcher, I just mean a pot or jar put outside that you can use each day to measure the rainfall. You could put markings on your jar or use a ruler to measure it. Either empty it at the end of the day ready for tomorrow or keep a running total (and note evaporation too!).

For a simpler—and braver—idea, dance in the rain!

# Beach

*<sup>14</sup> For the earth will be filled with the knowledge of  the*
     *glory of  the* LORD
     *as the waters cover the sea.*

                                        *Habakkuk 2:14*


*<sup>6</sup> For God, who said, "Let light shine out of  darkness,"*
*made his light shine in our hearts to give us the light of*
*the knowledge of  God's glory displayed in the face of*
*Christ.*

                                    *2 Corinthians 4:6*

# 10. THE CALM SEA
## Habakkuk 2:14; 2 Corinthians 4:6

Do you prefer to visit the beach in the cold stillness of a frosty day, or in blazing summer when the placid sea contrasts with the bustling beach? If the sea is calm, whatever else is going on, its vast depths occupy the entire horizon. Its immensity is profoundly calming—I love it just as much as I love playing in the waves. As a child, I enjoyed standing out on the deck of the ferry as our family set off across the sea toward Guernsey or France. My ideal was to find a view of the horizon with no land—just the rolling waves and maybe a ship in the distance.

Years later, I heard Habakkuk 2:14 and understood what those rolling waves of peace and calm were created to display. The waters cover the sea, and they do so to speak to us of the glory of God. I have made it a habit to say, at a first glimpse of the sea, "The earth will be filled with the knowledge of the glory of the LORD as the waters cover the sea." If it's warm enough to swim and the sea is peaceful, I like to walk into it until the water is up to my chin and look out so that my vision is entirely filled with the ocean. There, as the sun glints on the crystal surface, I see the glory of the Lord.

These are times when our hearts glimpse Christ more truly than usual. We are transported to the outer fringes of heaven and sense something of his glory. One day this glory will cover the entire earth as comprehensively as water covers the sea. So the sea speaks of the nature of God's glory. It is a calm and peaceful glory. It is a weighty and immense glory. It is glory that covers over any pretense of rival glories. It is a glory we can immerse ourselves in and swim through forever.

In 2 Corinthians 4:6, the writer, Paul, tells us that the glory of God is displayed in the face of Jesus Christ. It shines in the face that beckoned a woman by a Samaritan well into the kingdom of God—the face that looked up to Zacchaeus and called him home (John 4:1-42; Luke 19:1-10). This is the face that wept at the death of Lazarus and at the sin of Jerusalem (John 11:1-44; Luke 19:41-44). It is the face that turned toward heaven in a garden and said, "Not my will, but yours be done" (Luke 22:39-46). It is the face that was etched with pain and sorrow on the road to Calvary and still looked with forgiveness and love on a distraught mother, on gambling soldiers, on a desperate thief (John 19:17-27; Luke 23:39-43)—and on us.

The calm glory of the sea, filling east to west, north to south, is a promise from God that Christ's love, compassion, forgiveness and welcome will utterly flood the world. We will dive into that glory and swim free and laughing for all eternity. We will see his face, and Jesus will be smiling to us in welcome—telling us that he understands, that we are safe and that we are now home.

## FOR TODAY

Memorize Habakkuk 2:14. Then, when you see the sea, you can say it each time. And when you see Christ coming, you can say it as his glory floods the cosmos!

## FOR THE FAMILY

### Ask

- How much water do you think there is in the sea? When you look out to sea, what can you see? That much water is a picture of how God's glory will fill the world.
- Paul says we see God's glory in the face of Jesus. Can you think of someone in the Bible who met Jesus? What happened when they met him? How did he look at them or talk to them?

### Make

On the beach, gather seaweed, pebbles, driftwood or anything else you can find and use it to write the word "glory" on the sand. You could take a photo of this with the sea behind it. If you feel energetic, you could even write the whole of Habakkuk 2:14.

[35] *That day when evening came, he said to his disciples, "Let us go over to the other side." [36] Leaving the crowd behind, they took him along, just as he was, in the boat. There were also other boats with him. [37] A furious squall came up, and the waves broke over the boat, so that it was nearly swamped. [38] Jesus was in the stern, sleeping on a cushion. The disciples woke him and said to him, "Teacher, don't you care if we drown?"*

[39] *He got up, rebuked the wind and said to the waves, "Quiet! Be still!" Then the wind died down and it was completely calm.*

[40] *He said to his disciples, "Why are you so afraid? Do you still have no faith?"*

[41] *They were terrified and asked each other, "Who is this? Even the wind and the waves obey him!"*

*Mark 4:35-41*

# 11. THE WILD SEA

Mark 4:35-41

The sea is massively powerful. When a storm closes in on a seaside town, fishing boats are drawn up the beach and flood barriers slotted into place. There may be plenty of damage even so. To face such a mighty storm at sea is terrifying at another level. Even huge, modern ships are in danger.

Facing a storm in a small fishing boat would involve a desperate effort—the heavy oars hauled by tired men trying to keep the boat on course while their friends bail for their lives. This was how Jesus' disciples strove when a sudden squall swept down the Sea of Galilee. For all their skill and strength, the boat was nearly swamped. Now they turned to their Lord, waking him as their only hope. It seems as though they didn't quite know why they did so. They obviously expected *something*—he was more than simply another pair of hands. Just as obviously, though, they did not expect what he actually did!

What happened left them more terrified than when they were in the grip of the tempest. Jesus gave the waves a telling-off! He ordered them to be still. They obeyed him. Recognizing the voice that had called them from nothing into rolling existence all those years before, the very wind and waves were compelled to calm by the simple words of God. Christ's control of the natural world was total.

"Why are you so afraid?" Jesus' first question to the disciples was surprising. The reason for their fear was clear—they were facing death! His second question helps us to see why he asked it, though. If they had had faith in Jesus, they would have felt differently about the wind and waves. If they had really seen who was sleeping in the stern, they would have had no reason to fear the storm. Christ's absolute authority over wind and waves reveals that he is the Creator himself. Only God can rebuke a storm as we might rebuke a puppy! To see Jesus as God—the one who "rides on the wings of the wind" (Psalm 104:3)—is to see him rightly.

When we are unable to get our minds off the things that buffet and frighten us, we can remember Christ. We have no strength of our own against the winds and waves that come at us. Whether we look to the wider news or to our own circumstances, we may well be terrified. In Psalm 65:5-8 David compares the turmoil of the nations to the roaring of the seas. When mighty powers set themselves up against God, they resemble stormy seas—and they dismay us. Or in our personal lives we feel tossed to and fro by hardships and temptations. We know fear, worry, anxiety and even terror.

The only way out of this is to look to Christ. We wait for him to rebuke the storm. We do not wait in vain— he has already broken the dread of death and sin (Romans 6:1-11). We will have fears and even terrors to confront, but we will have Jesus too, and the one in the boat is far greater.

## FOR TODAY

Watch the might of the waves. Be respectful and amazed at their power, and imagine Jesus rebuking them. He is far greater, far more powerful. Fear the Lord, and then see what he does with your other fears.

## FOR THE FAMILY

### Ask

- What is fun about playing in the waves? Is it ever scary? Are there days when you would not dare to go near the sea? Life is a bit like that: often fun and a bit scary—sometimes terrifying. So…
- How can the story of Jesus calming the wind and waves help us to see who Jesus is? Once we see this, how can he help us when we are feeling scared?

### Chat

After spending some time watching the rough waves, talk together about the different things that are "waves" in your life. How can having "Jesus in the boat" make a difference to how you approach these "waves"?

*<sup>15</sup> The angel of the L*ORD *called to Abraham from heaven a second time <sup>16</sup> and said, "I swear by myself, declares the L*ORD*, that because you have done this and have not withheld your son, your only son, <sup>17</sup> I will surely bless you and make your descendants as numerous as the stars in the sky and as the sand on the seashore. Your descendants will take possession of the cities of their enemies, <sup>18</sup> and through your offspring all nations on earth will be blessed, because you have obeyed me."*

*Genesis 22:15-18*

# 12. SAND

Genesis 22:15-18

Today your task is to count the grains of sand on the beach!

No, I'm joking. Can you imagine trying to do that? Even approximating the number is beyond most of us.

The promise of the Lord to Abraham is staggering. The windswept sand pictures a greater salvation, and a greater Savior, than we usually expect. This is important as we consider our family and friends who do not follow Christ. I find it hard to persevere in praying for and sharing the gospel even with those I love. Years of hoping have dulled the edge of my efforts. Part of that might be a creeping sense that maybe the Lord is not quick to save. Maybe he is stingy in his rescue. Maybe he is reluctant, begrudging or slow.

When doubts about the willingness of Christ to save sinners gnaw at you, remember the beach. Remember how sandy it is. Then remember Abraham. Our Bible passage today comes just after he had displayed the depths of his faith in God, being prepared to obey the Lord's call to sacrifice Isaac, his son (Genesis 22:1-19). Isaac was the miracle-born son of Abraham and Sarah's old age. Isaac was the one through whom the Lord had said he would give them many descendants. Yet when God told Abraham to kill Isaac as a sacrifice,

Abraham obeyed. Hebrews 11:19 explains that he "considered that God was able even to raise [Isaac] from the dead" (ESV).

It was an astonishing act of faith. But God did not make Abraham follow through, instead providing a ram as a sacrifice in Isaac's place. Abraham had the wisdom to see that even this ram was not the ultimate sacrifice that was needed to take the place of his son. Something better was needed. There would be a better sacrifice and a greater rescue. Looking down the centuries, Abraham prophesied that there would be a sacrifice made on that very mountain, by which the Lord would truly provide salvation (Genesis 22:14).

Years later, Jesus would walk obediently up the very same mountain. This time the Lord himself was the Father—and he did not spare his own heart as he had spared Abraham's. He plunged the knife of judgment into the heart of the sinless Lamb. On the cross, Jesus provided a sacrifice sufficient to cover all our sins. He paid a price of infinite value to buy us out of our slavery to sin (Hebrews 9:28).

Is God reluctant to save? Ask Abraham.

Is God stingy in doling out salvation? Count the sand.

Have you given up on praying for those you love? The work of salvation cost Jesus everything; it cost the Father his Son. It was a mighty and hard work. It was a prophesied and planned work. It was a mighty salvation that could only flow out of a heart of staggering generosity and ever-expanding, boundless, amazing grace. You can pray with confidence that there will be as many of God's people as there are grains of sand on every beach in the world—and in hope that the ones you love will one day be numbered among them.

## FOR TODAY

Sand gets everywhere, doesn't it? It's in your pockets, in the upholstery of the car, in the luggage, in between your toes. Don't worry! The gritty feel of this sand in the months to come will remind you of this time away—and more importantly, it will remind you of the breadth of the salvation that Christ gives us.

## FOR THE FAMILY

### Ask

- Do you ever feel that there are not many Christians—that we are quite a lonely bunch? God says that his people will number more than the sand on the seashore. What do you think of that?
- What is good about being followers of Jesus? How could you help your friends enjoy the same things about Jesus?

### Make

Collect small pebbles, bits of sea-glass and shells from the beach. Then spend a few minutes praying for family and friends who do not yet follow Jesus. Each time you pray for someone, put a pebble in a jar. You can leave this jar out with the pile of pebbles next to it. Whenever you walk past, or at each meal, pray for someone and put a pebble in.

*¹ Hear my cry, O God;*
    *listen to my prayer.*

*² From the ends of the earth I call to you,*
    *I call as my heart grows faint;*
    *lead me to the rock that is higher than I.*
*³ For you have been my refuge,*
    *a strong tower against the foe.*

*⁴ I long to dwell in your tent forever*
    *and take refuge in the shelter of your wings,*
*⁵ For you, God, have heard my vows;*
    *you have given me the heritage of those who*
        *fear your name.*

*⁶ Increase the days of the king's life,*
    *his years for many generations.*
*⁷ May he be enthroned in God's presence forever;*
    *appoint your love and faithfulness to protect him.*

*⁸ Then I will ever sing in praise of your name*
    *and fulfill my vows day after day.*

*Psalm 61*

# 13. SANDCASTLES

Psalm 61

The sandcastle is a thing of wonder. It can be a turreted fable bedecked with paper flags and shells. Or it might look more like concrete fortifications—like the ones I used to make with my brother and my dad (sadly, we were not allowed to use actual concrete). Our aim was not prettiness but defense: we built strong walls, huge mounds and intricate moat systems. This was no joke. The threat faced by our sandcastles was immense. Obviously I knew that our castle was never really going to defeat the Atlantic—but there was always hope! And the fight was exhilarating. A truly worthy castle would still be standing, in a battered and sloppy fashion, long after the tide had forced us defenders to retreat up the beach for ice cream.

I loved making sandcastles with my dad, and I love making them with my own children. Even if they lose interest, I am still working hard as the tide comes in. My resolve to buttress and defend our castles is just as determined as I remember from my childhood—and the outcome just as inevitable.

The beauty and strength of these castles is short-lived. There is a joy to defending the forlorn hope of a sandcastle against the sea, but it would be no place to settle on as home. Spiritually speaking, too, there is only one truly strong tower and only one sufficiently high rock.

When I look at my life—my education, skills, money, possessions, family and friends—it can feel secure. I am the sort of person who likes plans, lists, schedules and structure. I like to be in control. I like to keep my defenses in good order. Maybe you do too. It does me good to watch, spade in hand, as the last of my castle walls is flattened by a retreating wave. There I see the truth about my life. Waves of ruin—illness, death, loss, betrayal and the folly of our own sin—crash down on us. If our trust is in ourselves, then we have built castles of sand.

This summer my family spent time away in the historic English city of Canterbury. There are so many reminders around the city of great figures—the authors Chaucer and Marlowe, for example, along with rich merchants and wise archbishops. These people commanded the power and resources of their day. None of them survived the surging tide. Time is eroding even their memory.

If we are to stand when these terrible waves come, it must be on a higher rock, taking refuge in a stronger tower. This is the sort of safety and security that Christ wants to give us. We cannot defend ourselves against the world, the flesh and the devil, nor against death itself. Jesus knows this. It is why he came to die and to rise. In his risen, invincible life we have our tower. In him we find our rock. To him we run for refuge.

## FOR TODAY

Build a sandcastle and defend it with every bit of strength you can muster—or smile at a job well done if you realize the tide is going out. Then celebrate all that it was with a befitting tribute (like ice cream). As you do so, let the Holy Spirit increase your joy as you think of how your life has been redeemed from such futility. This activity does not require children—trust me.

## FOR THE FAMILY

### Ask

- Which people and what things keep our family safe and secure?
- How does Jesus keep us safe and secure?

### Spot

This activity would obviously fit very well as the starting point for a discussion as a family. Another idea, though, might be to see who can spot the most sandcastles over the vacation. The first person to spot one gets a point. But you only get the point if you gesture toward it and shout, "Sandcastle! Jesus is a stronger tower!"

# Pool

*19 Therefore, brothers and sisters, since we have confidence to enter the Most Holy Place by the blood of Jesus, 20 by a new and living way opened for us through the curtain, that is, his body, 21 and since we have a great priest over the house of God, 22 let us draw near to God with a sincere heart and with the full assurance that faith brings, having our hearts sprinkled to cleanse us from a guilty conscience and having our bodies washed with pure water.*

*Hebrews 10:19-22*

# 14. COOL WATERS

Hebrews 10:19-22

There is great pleasure in prying your sun-baked self off the lounge chair, stepping up to the edge of the swimming pool and plunging into the cool water. It's a shock, but a delightful one, as the lethargy and heat are washed away. Such cool, cleansing, invigorating water is a picture of what happens when we come to Jesus. Our hearts and bodies are washed clean by his blood so that we are fit and ready to come before our God.

The background to this part of the book of Hebrews is the Old Testament temple and its system of sacrifices. This system was given by God to allow his people, Israel, to approach him. In the temple was the Most Holy Place, where the ark of the covenant rested behind a heavy curtain, cutting it off from the people. God's worshipers needed to be kept out of this section of the temple because God himself was enthroned on the "mercy seat" on top of the ark. A sinner who came into his holy presence was inviting destruction because the Lord is set against all evil. (For more on the sacrifices, see Leviticus 1 – 7; for more on the ark, the curtain and the holiness of the temple, see 1 Kings 8.)

Once a year, the high priest would make a sacrifice to atone for the sins of God's people. With blood in his hand and fear in his heart, he would step behind the curtain—surely wondering whether it would be the last step he would take. After all, Solomon's priests had been unable even to stand in the temple when the glory of the Lord filled it (1 Kings 8:10-11). Yet each high priest must also have been gripped with joy and awe at the prospect of entering into the presence of his Lord.

Then there came the day when a high priest gave *himself* as a sacrifice for his people. When Jesus, our great priest over the house of God, died, the curtain in the temple was torn in two from top to bottom (Mark 15:38-39). Jesus opened a way into the presence of God.

Now we do not approach with blood and terror. We approach God with the blood of Jesus and with confidence (Hebrews 10:19): with excitement, awe and the certainty that we will be welcomed, embraced and invited to come and sit and stay. The blood of Jesus has washed us clean. It is pure water to us.

This means that the swimming pool can be a picture of our life with Christ. Perhaps you remember how, before you became a follower of Jesus, you sometimes felt parched in your heart and soul. You had probably felt the harsh heat of suffering or the pain of toiling to create peace, hope and joy for yourself. When you began to follow Jesus, it may have felt like plunging into the refreshing waters of a pool. He gives us freely his love and kindness; he refreshes our souls. In him we can know the cool water of hope, even when the temperature of suffering is climbing high.

As well as reflecting on how the waters of the pool can help us appreciate the refreshment that Jesus gives our souls, think about what you tend to say to your friends by the pool. They may be dawdling at the edge, unsure whether to come in. But once you yourself have taken the plunge, you're quick to assure others, "It's lovely once you're in!" Well, so is our Lord! Let's pray that as we enjoy his reviving freshness, we would be just as quick to encourage others to join us in following him.

## FOR TODAY

Jump into the pool and relish the shock as the cold rushes over you. Laugh as you come up and delight in this picture of the life that Jesus gives you.

## FOR THE FAMILY

### Ask

- What is the best way of getting into the pool? Diving, jumping, sliding slowly down the steps? What is it like when you get into a pool for the first time that day?
- How can knowing Jesus feel similar to jumping into the pool?

### Do

How big a splash can you make when you jump into the pool? How small a ripple can you leave as you dive in and slip beneath the water? What games could you play in the pool, or how many lengths can you swim? Use the pool to the full range of its blessings today and keep in mind that it is an image of the life Christ gives you. What can this teach you about life?

# Hills &
# Mountains

¹ Then the LORD said to Moses, "Come up to the LORD, you and Aaron, Nadab and Abihu, and seventy of the elders of Israel. You are to worship at a distance…"

⁹ Moses and Aaron, Nadab and Abihu, and the seventy elders of Israel went up ¹⁰ and saw the God of Israel. Under his feet was something like a pavement made of lapis lazuli, as bright blue as the sky. ¹¹ But God did not raise his hand against these leaders of the Israelites; they saw God, and they ate and drank.

Exodus 24:1, 9-11

# 15. HEAVEN MEETS EARTH

Exodus 24:1, 9-11

In Scripture, mountains are often places where people meet God. Mount Zion, for example, is both a real place—the mountain on which Jerusalem (and the temple) was built—and an idea: a term to describe how God meets with and lives among his people. It's also called Mount Moriah (Genesis 22)—the place where God provided a sacrifice in the place of Isaac.

When we see and climb hills, we sense that we are closer to heaven. I used to dismiss this feeling as silly; being higher up cannot make much difference given how very high heaven must be. Noticing the significance of mountains in the Bible, and the encounters that God has with his people on their summits, has made me rethink. We can think of ourselves as going *up* to God in prayer, praise and love; there's a faithfulness in that. To climb a mountain can be a powerful reminder of Moses, Abraham and others doing the same as they went to meet God. And we can think of our Lord coming *down* to know us. We can have confidence that he will come down to meet us as we set our hearts on him.

A striking example of such a meeting is tucked away in Exodus 24. There is already an amazing closeness between God and his prophet Moses. In this meeting, though, the elders of Israel climb the mountain too.

It's the culmination of God's work in saving Israel from slavery in Egypt. Immediately before our verses, the Lord has committed himself to his people, and they have promised to obey the Lord and be faithful to him. Now the Lord calls the elders to come and feast in his great hall. They go up—and *see* God. They eat and drink with him. They go up the mountain and step into heaven; the gap is reduced to a single stride.

It was a special moment, not to be repeated. But standing on any mountain peak, between heaven and earth, should lift our eyes. It should remind us, above all, of the day when Jesus climbed up to Mount Zion, the mountain of his crucifixion. There God provided a feast of salvation for the world—a feast of bread and wine, a feast of his body and blood for us. Jesus climbed the hill to die for us, to take our guilt to heaven and to bring God's forgiveness to earth.

Standing on top of a mountain should remind us, then, that Jesus will come again to Mount Zion. On that day, he will come to it as the mountain of the Lord, the place of his return to earth, the venue for a greater feast (Zechariah 14:3-4; Acts 1:9-12; Revelation 19:6-10). One day—like Moses, Aaron, Nadab, Abihu, and the seventy elders of Israel—we will go up and see Jesus, the God of Israel. Under his feet will be a floor as bright blue as the sky (Revelation 4:1-6). Our God will not raise his hand against us; we will see God, and we will eat and drink. We will be home and need never leave that mountain, that feast, or that love.

## FOR TODAY

Before you climb the mountain, or as you look out over its grandeur, take time to pray that it will be a place where you will meet God. He won't come down physically as he did for Moses and others, but you can go up in faith. Climb the mountain of the Lord (Hebrews 12:22-24). Christ has granted you to do so.

## FOR THE FAMILY

### Ask

- What does it feel like when you are up a mountain or hill? Why do you think it feels that way?
- How could we use our hill walk today to help us worship God together?

### Do

As you climb today, if you have a step counter or phone app, why not keep an eye on how many steps you're doing and stop every 1,000 steps to say a prayer (maybe with a small snack!)? Pray about what you've read in this study or simply say thank you. Pray that the Lord will draw you all closer to himself as you draw closer to the summit. If you have a way of measuring it, you could stop every 100 feet climbed instead—or just every half hour.

When you get home, see if you can find out how high you climbed and compare it with these mountains: Mount Everest: 29,032 feet above sea level. Mont Blanc: 15,774 feet. Mount Kilimanjaro: 19,341 feet. Mount Sinai: 7,497 feet. Mount Zion: 2,510 feet.

*<sup>31</sup> Jeroboam built shrines on high places and appointed priests from all sorts of people, even though they were not Levites. <sup>32</sup> He instituted a festival on the fifteenth day of the eighth month, like the festival held in Judah, and offered sacrifices on the altar. This he did in Bethel, sacrificing to the calves he had made. And at Bethel he also installed priests at the high places he had made. <sup>33</sup> On the fifteenth day of the eighth month, a month of his own choosing, he offered sacrifices on the altar he had built at Bethel. So he instituted the festival for the Israelites and went up to the altar to make offerings.*

*1 Kings 12:31-33*

# 16. FALSE WORSHIP

1 Kings 12:31-33

As we worship Christ on the mountains, we must not lose sight of the false worship sometimes given in such places. In today's passage, King Jeroboam is presuming to do what only God can do. The "high places" of Israel were shrines originally set up for the worship of the Lord, but then converted to the worship of other gods. Actually, though, they were never legitimate places to worship God—that was only the tabernacle or temple. Jeroboam is trying to make the worship of God something he controls, for his own blessing. He is usurping God's authority, and it will result in false worship.

We should go to meet God in his appointed place. For us, that is no longer a building. The "place" where we now meet God is actually a person: Jesus Christ. Christ is our temple: the Son of God, who became flesh and pitched his tabernacle among us (John 1:14).

Hills, beaches, sunsets and stars are meant to magnify our worship of Christ. They are created by him as shards of his glory, glimpses of his holiness. This makes them particularly dangerous, as they can easily replace him. When I was given my first car, a silver Mini Cooper, as a total surprise, I was so captivated by the wonder, beauty and promise of the gift that I almost forgot my mom and dad, who had given it to me! Likewise, things which reflect Jesus are so full of wonder and glory that we can be dazzled. We start worshiping the wrong thing.

Plenty of religions have made gods of the sun or moon, of the hill or mountain. Today our friends might scoff at such ideas; yet so many of them live for travel and for experiences in creation—surfing, swimming, running, climbing, cycling, and endless other activities. The cult of leisure and experience is growing, with its priesthood of YouTube stars, its religious paraphernalia of ever-lighter bikes or more sophisticated running trainers, and its priestly garments of Lycra or technologically advanced wicking fabric.

Our relationship with God is direct: we are loved by and love Jesus. We can enjoy creation (with ever-greater wonder and joy) as a gift. Or we can enjoy the creation apart from him. We can receive the blessings and forget the fount of all blessing. If we do, we will find that the blessings become a curse. Apart from Jesus, all our little gods become demons. The glorious sunset run becomes a bitter disappointment when you realize your time is poor. Surfing ceases to be fun when others aren't impressed by your skill. The thirst for new and exciting destinations can suck your time and energy and stop you enjoying your regular life.

Jesus is the awesome Creator and generous Lord, and so we must always let his creation and gifts point us back to him, in case we turn to adore them instead. The way we do so is very simple: we give thanks. We receive gifts as gifts—with gratitude in our hearts and on our lips to the Giver, who is far greater than his gifts. This is why I wrote this book! I love creation, and I love time away in creation—and I hate the way my heart twists away from Christ and squeezes the joy out of so much beauty. I want to learn, once again and more deeply, to give thanks.

## FOR TODAY
Give thanks!

## FOR THE FAMILY
### Ask

- What have you most enjoyed about where we are staying so far?
- What are you most looking forward to? Let's spend some time thanking God for all these good gifts.

### Make

Take a sheet of paper to make a thank you list. Write "Thank you Jesus" at the top in decorated letters, and then begin a list of the things you are grateful for. Add to this throughout your trip, and maybe when you get home too. You could put it up on a kitchen cupboard or tuck it into your Bible.

<sup>18</sup> *"Come now, let us settle the matter,"*
*says the* LORD.
*"Though your sins are like scarlet,*
*they shall be as white as snow;*
*though they are red as crimson,*
*they shall be like wool.*
<sup>19</sup> *If you are willing and obedient,*
*you will eat the good things of the land;*
<sup>20</sup> *but if you resist and rebel,*
*you will be devoured by the sword."*
*For the mouth of the* LORD *has spoken.*

*Isaiah 1:18-20*

# 17. SNOWY PEAKS

Isaiah 1:18-20

Snow transforms everything. The humblest hill becomes a shimmering mound. As I write, we have had an unusually prolonged period of snowy weather in our part of England. Halfway through a hitherto extremely wet winter, I went to bed expecting the next day to be just as muddy, dull and slushy. Then I woke, and the dawn glittered with pure whiteness. The mud was gone, the drenched bushes frozen into jeweled statues.

When we ascend to the snow-covered hills—with ski goggles on, or pulling a toboggan, or hiking in the early spring—we are shown a picture of how our sin is utterly covered up with the pure righteousness of Jesus. The sins are red, scarlet and crimson before God; we cannot sponge them out (Isaiah 1:18). Maybe it's not too much of a stretch to say that they are also muddy. Our sins are grimy, drab and pathetic as well as stark, wicked and terrible.

To live for myself (that's essentially what sin is) is at times to treat God and others with terrible cruelty and disdain. I can treat people as if they were objects instead of as those who bear the image of the divine Creator. These sins are the ones that are "like scarlet." They cry out for justice. At other times, my selfishness, ingratitude and unkindness are low-level and grumbling. These sins are no less serious, but they seem more muddy than red.

Either way, our sin can be covered over as if by snow (Psalm 51:7). When Christ died, he washed away our sin (Titus 3:3-7). To be saved by Jesus is to be cleaned by Jesus. Strangely, though, he does not restore us to some pre-sin state of innocence. No, his cleansing leaves us shining in radiant glory in a way that is more than merely sinless (Ephesians 5:25-27). He shares with us his own perfect righteousness (Romans 3:21-24). He not only drains the cup of judgment we deserve; he fills it with the finest wine (Matthew 26:27, 39).

We are covered with Christ's purity and goodness in the same way the hills are blanketed with snow, leaving them more beautiful than they were to start with. Dazzling righteousness—which Jesus has by virtue of both his character and his deeds—is given to us. The snow-covered mountains stand as a picture of the people of Jesus. This goodness of Jesus is ours to have and enjoy and ponder, and we come to our Father not as sinners set against his love but as children clothed in the righteousness of Christ.

This means that now we live as the righteous ones of God. We are given righteous acts to do, godly choices to make, costly sacrifices to give and lives of love to live. We are given God's Spirit to enable us to live this way (Hebrews 9:13-14). No longer must we live ashamed of our sins, whether they're scarlet or muddy. No longer must we try to cover them up by our own efforts. Now we are covered by Christ's righteousness as the snow lies over the hills. We live out this righteousness in daily lives of love toward God and our neighbors. When we fail, and sin again, we don't need to worry: Jesus has plenty of snowy righteousness to cover it over once more.

## FOR TODAY

Snow is great fun to play in, hike through, or ski down. Today, though, take a few moments to simply stand in its stillness and enjoy the peace and glory that it brings. This is like the peace and glory of our forgiven life, of the delightful outworking in us of the death of Christ for us.

## FOR THE FAMILY

### Ask

- What do you think the snow is covering? How would things look without it?
- This is a picture of how Jesus covers over our sins with his righteousness. How different might we be if he did not do that?

### Spot

See who can spot the tallest snow-covered peak, the deepest snow drift or the strangest snow-covered shape. As you play your spotting game, chat about how different we are because Christ has made us as clean as the snow.

# Forests

*¹ Then the angel showed me the river of the water of life, as clear as crystal, flowing from the throne of God and of the Lamb ² down the middle of the great street of the city. On each side of the river stood the tree of life, bearing twelve crops of fruit, yielding its fruit every month. And the leaves of the tree are for the healing of the nations. ³ No longer will there be any curse. The throne of God and of the Lamb will be in the city, and his servants will serve him. ⁴ They will see his face, and his name will be on their foreheads. ⁵ There will be no more night. They will not need the light of a lamp or the light of the sun, for the Lord God will give them light. And they will reign forever and ever.*

*Revelation 22:1-5*

# 18. TREES OF LIFE

Revelation 22:1-5

Trees surely whisper to one another! When we wander through ancient woodland—particularly those of us who wish we lived in Middle-Earth or Narnia—we have a sense that we are wandering through the years. These lofty boughs and soaring trunks may, as saplings, have witnessed hunting parties and fugitives, grand ladies and weary travelers. Trees speak of growth, fruitfulness, shade, rest and healing. They speak through the years. "When through the woods and forest glades I wander ... Then sings my soul, my Savior God to thee, how great thou art!" (Carl Boberg; translated from the Russian by Stuart K. Hine).

Eden was a garden with two particularly special trees: the tree of life and the tree of the knowledge of good and evil (Genesis 2:9). The first tree spoke of God's generous gifts. God had created Adam and Eve to stroll unashamed at his side in the cool of the day. This tree's fruit gave a life of freedom and love, peace and joy, service and wonder.

But Adam and Eve abandoned this life when they ate from the second tree (Genesis 3:1-7). God had forbidden them to eat from the tree of the knowledge of good and evil (Genesis 2:16-17). Yet, when Satan whispered in their ears, they began to disbelieve and distrust God.

This wonderful tree became a tree of death: as they ate, they severed their friendship and partnership with God and abandoned their worship of him. They died in their spirits and became subject to death in their bodies. They could have lived with God in the garden for all eternity, but they were to perish east of Eden (Genesis 3:22-24).

It might have ended there. They had grasped and snatched at equality with God. They deserved to be strung up on that very tree, hanging cursed between heaven and earth. Instead they were made to leave the garden. They were banished from the tree of life—but that tree was not uprooted.

Years later God came to another garden, on a hill covered with olive trees. In the cool of the day, Jesus met with his friends there. In that garden, one of those friends betrayed him with a kiss, and Jesus was led to a tree of death (Matthew 26:36 – 27:50). Not all trees are good! On the cross, that hideous tree, our Savior hung—crowned with branches of thorns—and died.

Dying on death's tree, Jesus broke death's power. It no longer has any hold over us. Death has become, in the bursting light of Easter morning, no longer a tomb but a tunnel. We pass through death, in all its pain and sorrow, and come out blinking and smiling into the light of the welcome in Jesus' face (1 Corinthians 15:53-56). The tree of death has been felled. When Christ returns, there will only be one tree in the new Jerusalem: a tree of life, heavy with fruit and healing leaves (Revelation 22:2).

God hung on the tree of death in our place—and so it is right that the leafy boughs of a quiet forest whisper life to our souls. Jesus tasted death for us, and so we will not have to chew that bitter fruit. The only fruit left for us to taste is the fruit of the tree of life.

## FOR TODAY
Take a quiet moment to let the trees, these living monuments, direct your gaze and heart to the Lord, who came to die on a cross so that we might live in the shade and protection of a greater tree.

## FOR THE FAMILY
### Ask
- How do you feel when you are walking in the woods on a sunny afternoon?
- The Bible says that when Jesus comes back, there will be a tree of life, with leaves that heal. How will it feel to sit in the shade of a tree like that?

### Spot
Who can spot the tallest tree? The smallest? The one with the widest trunk? If you all link arms, can you get all the way round it? As you have fun with this huge tree, talk together about what the tree of life will look like. How tall will it be? How wide and leafy? What flowers or fruit will you see in its branches? And how might it be decorated?

<sup>25</sup> *"Therefore I tell you, do not worry about your life, what you will eat or drink; or about your body, what you will wear. Is not life more than food, and the body more than clothes?* <sup>26</sup> *Look at the birds of the air; they do not sow or reap or store away in barns, and yet your heavenly Father feeds them. Are you not much more valuable than they?"*

*Matthew 6:25-26*

# 19. CONSIDER THE BIRDS

## Matthew 6:25-26

We spend so much time worrying. We bring those worries away with us, hoping to quiet them in the peace and fun of time away; yet sometimes the quiet just means they scream more loudly. Some of those worries are very real—a job under threat, a serious illness, or a complex problem in our family or among our friends. Some fears are less real—but no less terrifying.

I struggle with mild anxiety and have several close friends who are gripped by a more vicious version. Mine means both that I feel overly anxious about specific concerns and that I carry a general sense of anxiety that has no specific grounds. I find myself in a cottage or cabin somewhere, the day spreading before me with possibilities; and I am worrying that if I don't do the washing up straight away, then it might not get done until evening. I'm not even sure what would be so bad about that, but it fills me with anxious dread. I can laugh at myself in hindsight, but it feels serious at the time.

One reason we might be anxious is because we are not in control of our lives. Away from home, as we miss the comforting sense of security brought by familiar rhythms of daily life, we become even more aware that we are not really in charge. Perhaps you have sought solace in a quiet walk only to find that when you leave your tent or cottage and head into the woods, the worries and fears compete with one another more than ever, clamoring for your attention.

But the birds sing with carefree exuberance. Mere sparrows can drown out the clamor of our worries. How? Because the birds—if you listen with Jesus' words in Matthew 6 in mind—sing of how deeply your Father loves you, and how mightily he cares for you.

Do these birds not worry? Surely they should! They have no store cupboards of food. They're wasting time making music, frittering away their lives. Why are they not more urgent, more focused, more productive? It's because they have learned that they are precious in God's sight and he will feed them (Matthew 6:26). Are you not much more valuable than they? As your heavenly Father gazes down even now, does his heart not rest on you with love and delight? He loves you, and he is in control. He is the one who sees the end from the beginning (Isaiah 46:10). He knows how it will work out, and he works all things for our good (Romans 8:28). All things.

This will probably not be enough to relieve your worries instantly, though. So let's remember together that Jesus is Lord, our Father is kind, and his Spirit is close—and they love you. Even when we feel controlled by our anxieties, there is no change to God's love. Our Father does not tell us to "just stop worrying"; instead he sits by our side through the night until we hear the birds singing at the first light of dawn.

## FOR TODAY

Listen to the birds sing. Learn their lesson again, until your worries are neither masked nor hidden but have shrunk back to the size they should be in the face of an immense and eternal love.

## FOR THE FAMILY

### Ask

- What sorts of things would you worry about if you were a bird? What is it about God that means the birds have plenty of time for singing beautiful songs?
- What can we do to be like the birds?

### Do

Who can make the best bird noises? Try to imitate the call or song of a bird you can hear and see who does it best. As you talk about the bird, you might even be able to identify some of them on an app. What can you see about how the birds are behaving that can teach you more about trusting God?

# Farmland

*⁵ What, after all, is Apollos? And what is Paul? Only servants, through whom you came to believe – as the Lord has assigned to each his task. ⁶ I planted the seed, Apollos watered it, but God has been making it grow. ⁷ So neither the one who plants nor the one who waters is anything, but only God, who makes things grow. ⁸ The one who plants and the one who waters have one purpose, and they will each be rewarded according to their own labor. ⁹ For we are co-workers in God's service; you are God's field, God's building.*

*1 Corinthians 3:5-9*

# 20. FARMERS AND FARMHANDS

1 Corinthians 3:5-9

Farming is an uncertain business, dependent on weather and soil, insects and climate. Think of the workers on a farm early in the year. They will be repairing fences, cutting hedges, plowing fields and drilling seed—working hard together. They won't all view their work in the same way, though.

The farmer organizes, manages and directs the labors of his farmhands. He has the extra responsibility of reading the soil and the weather to determine which tasks in the endless list should be done today and which tomorrow. He shoulders the burden of the farm. It is the farmer who has to work out how to sleep amid the stresses of spreadsheets, animal diseases, market fluctuations and weather reports.

At the end of the day, the farmhand rolls into bed with aching muscles and the prospect of a full pay packet, with a bit extra folded in by a fair boss who noticed the long hours. In a distant way he might be concerned by the same matters as the farmer. It would be strange, though, for him to stay up late poring over spreadsheets or to lose sleep because of an unfavorable forecast.

How often do we try to shoulder responsibility that is the Lord's alone? We do it in our work, in our family life and among our friends. The particular focus of our passage today, though, is the church. Paul's point is that in the Lord's fields we are only servants. By the generosity of our God, we are his fellow-workers. He shares his work with us, equipping us by his Spirit to sow and reap as the season demands. The mistake we make is to think that we share God's responsibility for the work.

Whether we carry out some officially recognized ministry or simply serve where and as we can, it is easy for us to feel the need to calculate the impact of our service. It's not wrong to consider the numbers who came, the feedback we received, or the comments from the pastor. Yet we must recognize that only the Lord is able to give the spiritual life and growth that our church family and our neighbors need. These things are what matter most—but they rest in people's hearts and they cannot be counted. The danger is that we tend to prioritize the less important things which *can* be counted.

The Lord takes responsibility. We might plant or we might water, but if there is growth, then it is the Lord who gave it, not us. This frees us from pride's bitter slavery. We need not worry about the "success" of the ministry. God will reward us according to our labors. He sees the prayer for the children in the Sunday School; he observes the late-night study for tomorrow's community group. He notices the love that drew you to stop by to see a sick friend or write a note to a grieving relative. The Lord gives us good works to walk in. He delights as we stride along the farm track at his side to gather in the harvest he has grown.

At times like these, when you are away from your

everyday service of God, why not pray for those you left at home? As you do so, take time to give thanks that the Lord is working even as you are resting. He gives us both meaningful work and rest, partly to help us remember that he is the one who shoulders the responsibility.

## FOR TODAY

Consider the beauty and abundance of the fields as a picture of the world in God's sight. You may not see growth, but God sees what is happening under the ground. He knows the quality of the corn. You are in his hands, and he knows how to farm.

## FOR THE FAMILY

### Ask

- Do you think it would be fun to work on a farm? What sorts of things do you think you would get to do?
- What do you think it is like to work in God's "farm," his church?

### Spot

Spot tractors. If you see one first, you get a point. If it is moving, you get an extra point. One more for a trailer. Maybe three points for a combine. Or work out your own more elaborate scoring system. (Red ones should probably get an extra point!) If you see a teleporter, you get ten points as long as you say, "Beam me up, Scotty." (And if you didn't know that farmers had teleporters, do an internet search—I'm not joking!)

*¹ When the* L<small>ORD</small> *restored the fortunes of Zion,*
  *we were like those who dreamed.*
*² Our mouths were filled with laughter,*
  *our tongues with songs of joy.*
*Then it was said among the nations,*
  *"The* L<small>ORD</small> *has done great things for them."*
*³ The* L<small>ORD</small> *has done great things for us,*
  *and we are filled with joy.*

*⁴ Restore our fortunes,* L<small>ORD</small>,
  *like streams in the Negev.*
*⁵ Those who sow with tears*
  *will reap with songs of joy.*
*⁶ Those who go out weeping,*
  *carrying seed to sow,*
*will return with songs of joy,*
  *carrying sheaves with them.*

*Psalm 126*

# 21. SOWING AND REAPING

Psalm 126

We long for fruitfulness. We were created by God to work and serve his kingdom. Sometimes, frankly, we just long to see some results. The point of this psalm is that, wonderfully, God gives the growth, and we merely sow his fields. "Sowing" language is sometimes used specifically of Bible teaching or sharing the gospel; in this psalm it seems to be used more widely, about all the good we seek to do and establish.

Often, though, we sow with tears. Tears at decades of seeming fruitlessness; tears at the painful labor of sowing. Tears because so little seems to have grown or because everything is burning down. Maybe tears when a longed-for trip away proves to be bitterly disappointing.

Sometimes the tears are anxious. We seek to sow wisdom, wonder and the gospel itself in the lives of our children, for example. We long to see the first shoots of these plants growing, but we are worried some days that there seem to be more weeds than wheat. Maybe we labor long hours, working and studying to progress in our career, yet we see how fickle advancement is and how slow.

Sometimes the tears are bitter. We have seen everything we worked for turn to dust. A hard-won and long-established reputation is trashed in hours. The family we poured everything into is ripped apart by divorce, death or estrangement. A good job is lost by a stupid mistake. Why did God let this happen?

We want the tears to stop. We might decide to guard our hearts more carefully. Stay safe; look after number one; do not take risks. But there is a better way. We can keep sowing in tears. We can keep taking the seed the Lord gives us—seeds of love and truth—and go out again to sow and to weep. By the grace of God, we can realize that the tears are not always to be avoided; they are part of the sowing. They are essential to the harvest.

The tears of the faithful sower are never wasted. Jesus wept at the grave of Lazarus, his friend (John 11:33-36). He wept over Jerusalem, his city (Luke 19:41). Jesus sowed in tears. But here is the hope: just as we are called to suffer in Christ's image, so we will share in his harvest. The end of the tears will come on the day of the harvest. Verse 6 is one to learn by heart! We will be given songs to sing, joy to lift our heads and Jesus to lead us home.

A farmer friend once asked me, "Who wouldn't want to work on a farm during harvest?" I was riding beside him in his combine harvester and, yes, seriously considering a career change! That was a good day. Another friend, years ago, told me about a harvest she experienced as a child before the First World War—describing how her father lifted her onto the wagon as he led the cart horse home with a full load. That was a good day too, its memory still fresh after 80 years.

We are looking forward to a better day, though. Do not stop sowing. The Lord sees your tears. Do not stop sowing, for there will be a harvest greater than you can imagine. Do not stop sowing, for you work, and weep, alongside Jesus.

## FOR TODAY

What is hard about being a farmer? And how does this map onto your sufferings and struggles? And what is it like to be in the fields ripe for harvest? How do you think the farmer feels then, among that wind-rippled abundance?

## FOR THE FAMILY
### Ask

- What do you think it is like to be a farmer during the harvest? What would you be doing, and how would you be feeling?
- God's love and truth are a bit like seeds. They are sown in our hearts as we learn about Jesus in the Bible and live in a church family. What would it look like for this sort of seed to grow and produce more seeds? How does Jesus feel as he harvests this crop?

### Make

There are few better ways to appreciate harvest than by eating freshly baked bread together! You could buy some fresh from a local baker or find some part-baked bread rolls to put in an oven—or go the whole way, type "easy white bread rolls" into a search engine and follow the recipe. Then eat them warm with lots of butter!

*¹ The* LORD *is my shepherd, I lack nothing.*
*² He makes me lie down in green pastures,*
*he leads me beside quiet waters,*
*³ he refreshes my soul.*
*He guides me along the right paths*
*for his name's sake.*
*⁴ Even though I walk*
*through the darkest valley,*
*I will fear no evil,*
*for you are with me;*
*your rod and your staff,*
*they comfort me.*

*⁵ You prepare a table before me*
*in the presence of my enemies.*
*You anoint my head with oil;*
*my cup overflows.*
*⁶ Surely your goodness and love will follow me*
*all the days of my life,*
*and I will dwell in the house of the* LORD
*forever.*

*Psalm 23 (A psalm of David)*

# 22. SHEPHERDING

Psalm 23

Sheep are not impressive creatures. They are known for being silly, unaware of danger and prone to wandering off. They are experts at getting out of their fields onto the road; and terrible at getting back in! In some places they are kept safe by rigorous fencing. In many others their only hope is their shepherd.

We once had a summer break in a croft on the west coast of Scotland. Apart from two walkers, the only other person to pass within our sight during the week was a shepherd, expertly guiding his flock across a rocky and treacherous stretch of coastline. Those sheep reflect us: our only hope is our Shepherd, Jesus Christ.

David, the writer of Psalm 23, was a shepherd himself—both literally in his early life and metaphorically as the shepherd-king of Israel. He knew what he was writing about. Yet he does not elevate himself alongside the Lord; there is no "us shepherds" here. David is content to be a needy sheep. As a sheep he depends on the Lord to take him to good pasture, to let him know when it is safe for him to lie down, and to lead him to water. He, like us, needs a clear-sighted shepherd with a steady gaze to lead him.

Sometimes, though, we need our Shepherd to do

more than lead us. Even a silly sheep like me knows that there are wolves around. Sometimes we feel the darkness, and the chill rises. Sorrow and pain stalk us, and fear and dread are close. For some of us this psalm is a hard one to read because we heard it at the funeral of a very dear one. It breaks our hearts to read it again. But your Shepherd draws close. As you sense the danger and as distress approaches, his staff nudges you. A kind word and a touch of comfort gives warmth and light that cannot be overcome. You glance up and see that your Shepherd is smiling at you. Yet his gaze isn't only fixed on you.

As he steps away, you catch the scent of the wolf. You see your Shepherd's hand fit a stone to his sling. He runs toward the wolf as he swings his shot. There are two ways the shepherd seeks to save the sheep. He hopes his aim is true, but, in case it isn't, he gets between the wolf and its prey. David set himself between the giant and God's people (1 Samuel 17); his God-steadied aim was true and the sheep were saved. Years later, Christ our Shepherd set himself between sin and his people; his God-steadied aim was true, and the sheep were saved.

The Shepherd gave his life for his sheep (John 10:1-12). As a result, his feast is set out ready for us: Christ has gone to prepare a place for us in the house of the Lord, where we will dwell forever (John 14:2). Jesus is the Good Shepherd, who leads us well. He is before and beside us through the darkness. We are the sheep of his pasture.

## FOR TODAY

This psalm seems to grow in beauty when read aloud slowly. Do that now and let the Spirit guide the eyes of your heart to that Good Shepherd's care of you, his sheep.

## FOR THE FAMILY

### Ask

- What are sheep like? What do they do, and how do they act? How are we like them?
- What are shepherds like? What do they do, and how do they act? How is Jesus like them?

### Spot

Why not count sheep? You may like to do a tally if you are in hill-farming country or on a sheep farm. You could set a target for the afternoon. You could count shepherds too and, if you are passing one, start a conversation about a shepherd's life and what sheep are like. If there aren't many sheep where you are, set a drawing or a making challenge. What can you collect today that you could make into a model sheep? Or who can draw the best sheep with their eyes closed?

# Cities

*<sup>29</sup> …as [King Nebuchadnezzar] was walking on the roof of the royal palace of Babylon, <sup>30</sup> he said, "Is not this the great Babylon I have built as the royal residence, by my mighty power and for the glory of my majesty?"*

*<sup>31</sup> Even as the words were on his lips, a voice came from heaven, "This is what is decreed for you, King Nebuchadnezzar: Your royal authority has been taken from you. <sup>32</sup> You will be driven away from people and will live with the wild animals; you will eat grass like the ox. Seven times will pass by for you until you acknowledge that the Most High is sovereign over all kingdoms on earth and gives them to anyone he wishes."*

*<sup>33</sup> Immediately what had been said about Nebuchadnezzar was fulfilled. He was driven away from people and ate grass like the ox. His body was drenched with the dew of heaven until his hair grew like the feathers of an eagle and his nails like the claws of a bird.*

*<sup>34</sup> At the end of that time, I, Nebuchadnezzar, raised my eyes toward heaven, and my sanity was restored. Then I praised the Most High; I honored and glorified him who lives forever.*

*Daniel 4:29-34*

# 23. GREAT BABYLON

Cities seduce us. They stand as testimony to the glory and power of humanity—like proud Babylon, whose splendor, strength and beauty were legendary throughout the ancient world. Babylon's majesty had been crafted by its king. Nebuchadnezzar's power was vast. He had led the armies that brought in the wealth of conquered nations. He had passed the laws that created a prosperous society. He had employed the architects, landscapers and planners who had made his city magnificent.

This had not led to a proper sense of wonder and awe, though. The king of Babylon knew about God, since the Lord had led him to appoint faithful Daniel as his chief minister (Daniel 1:18-20; 2:47). As this all-conquering monarch surveyed all that he had been given to achieve, he should have knelt in gratitude and praise to God, who is King over all kings. Instead his heart swelled with pride, and he spoke his own praise and glory, just as Daniel had fearlessly prophesied a year before (Daniel 4:4-28). Then another voice rang out.

The one in heaven is far greater. He is not merely high or higher—he is *Most High*. He had given Nebuchadnezzar his crown, and he could just as easily remove it. This was what he now did. Along with the crown, he removed the king's sense and his dignity. It was a terrible punishment: here was the most powerful man on earth on all fours, his hair long, matted and scraggly, grazing like an ox. (Try looking up William Blake's painting *Nebuchadnezzar* to get a vivid idea of what it was like.)

Cities can seduce us, but they can also draw us to Christ. Jerusalem, after all, stood to the glory of God. The challenge of cities is to remember the source of their glory: it flows from a gracious God, through those he made in his image. God is the "painter" of all that we see. There is a higher artist behind every amazing picture, every glorious cathedral. We praise the architect, planner and gardener, and we praise the governments, kings and leaders who set them at their work. We must not stop there. We praise God, who gave the human architects their skill and the kings their thrones. All the good we see in a city has been achieved by creatures made in the image of God.

Humbled, Nebuchadnezzar repented. This is a deeply surprising and amazing conversion. In his kindness, the Lord humbled this arrogant monarch, and he responded with a beautiful faith. He no longer gazed at Babylon; instead his eyes were turned toward heaven, where the throne of the Most High is set in a far greater city. As you wander an earthly city today, may the beauty and majesty you see draw your eyes heavenward to contemplate the beauty and majesty of the King of kings, from whom all beauty and majesty flows.

## FOR TODAY

Give due praise to those responsible for the beauty and glory of the city. Let your eyes be drawn to the majesty and your heart inspired by the strength and confidence you see in a city. Then give due praise to the one who appointed those kings, who is the Most High and whose heavenly city is exceedingly splendid.

## FOR THE FAMILY
### Ask

- How do you feel as we see the magnificent buildings and beautiful parts of the city?
- Would you like to live in a city like this? One day we will live in God's city; what do you think that will be like?

### Spot

Look out for the most beautiful view, grandest building or tallest tower. This would be a good day to take lots of selfies and then compare them at the end of the day. Who got the best one and spotted the best sights?

*²² Paul then stood up in the meeting of the Areopagus [the ruling council in ancient Athens] and said: "People of Athens...*

*²⁴ "The God who made the world and everything in it is the Lord of heaven and earth and does not live in temples built by human hands. ²⁵ And he is not served by human hands, as if he needed anything. Rather, he himself gives everyone life and breath and everything else. ²⁶ From one man he made all the nations, that they should inhabit the whole earth; and he marked out their appointed times in history and the boundaries of their lands. ²⁷ God did this so that they would seek him and perhaps reach out for him and find him, though he is not far from any one of us. ²⁸ 'For in him we live and move and have our being.' As some of your own poets have said, 'We are his offspring.'*

*²⁹ "Therefore since we are God's offspring, we should not think that the divine being is like gold or silver or stone—an image made by human design and skill. ³⁰ In the past God overlooked such ignorance, but now he commands all people everywhere to repent. ³¹ For he has set a day when he will judge the world with justice by the man he has appointed. He has given proof of this to everyone by raising him from the dead."*

*Acts 17:22, 24-31*

# 24. TEMPLES

Acts 17:22, 24-31

In cities we pass many temples. Some are erected to named gods of other religions. Others stand to the glory of gods such as money or power. The columns and arches of our great shopping malls emulate Roman temples. Mere things take on personalities as brands that offer to fulfill our dreams and hopes. Although we are created to give praise to the Lord, we so often worship stand-in gods instead.

Strangely, the majesty of their temples shows us the fragility of these gods. They need our fine work, our silver and gold, our praise and attention. Without it they cease to be: a famous department store closes or a once-great religion is forgotten.

As we observe the worship of the city, we can emulate Paul in seeing that the essential desire here is right. Those who do not know Jesus are still created for joyful, awe-filled worship. If they do not direct that impulse to the Lord of life, they will direct it to a god of wood or stone: the latest products of a technology company or the fabulously dressed mannequins of the best fashion brands. When you pass a gorgeously proportioned temple in Bangkok, and perhaps also when you visit a sleekly presented flagship store in New York, you see a beautiful impulse twisted.

We get to untwist it. We get to affirm all that is good, useful and right in such an enterprise, while utterly rejecting the worship of anything other than our Lord. We can let our hearts be drawn to worship the one who does not need such displays of power. Like Paul, we can be those who worship a higher Lord and call others to join us. God does not need our buildings or our service. He is the one who made and owns all things.

With the beautiful cathedrals and church buildings that adorn many cities, we need to be nuanced. Often they speak to the "glory" of a church greedy for worldly power. But they also display the skills of masons made in God's image, used in worshipful work. As such we should bow our heads in remembering that the magnificence of these church buildings does not approach the worth of such a God as Jesus. The best of their builders, as they forged crosses for their spires and carved them on their pulpits, knew this.

The Lord of glory is content to dwell nowhere lower than heaven above. No temple could approach his splendor. Strangely, though, he did not despise a manger in Bethlehem or a cross outside Jerusalem. Jesus is God's appointed judge to bring justice to the nations (Acts 17:31) and, splendid though they are, none of the temples or church buildings you see today will stand. The new Jerusalem will not need a temple (Revelation 21:22): our Father and his Son will be her temple, and her streets will be filled with his Spirit.

## FOR TODAY

Write out Paul's description of God and his lack of need for human temples. Put it in your pocket so that all day it will help you to prayerfully remember how much greater our Lord is than the gods worshiped in this city.

## FOR THE FAMILY

### Ask

- Jesus did not always live in heaven. Where else do you remember him being?
- What do you think it was like for Jesus to live in a normal family in a town on earth when he was used to the splendor of heaven?

### Chat

As you walk around the city with your child or children, look out for something that shows the greatness of a person, like a ruler's palace. Then talk together about how you might tell a friend about the greatness of Jesus, using that as a starting point. You are trying to do what Paul did in our Bible passage.

²² The Israelites said to Gideon, "Rule over us—you, your son and your grandson—because you have saved us from the hand of Midian."

²³ But Gideon told them, "I will not rule over you, nor will my son rule over you. The LORD will rule over you." ²⁴ And he said, "I do have one request, that each of you give me an earring from your share of the plunder." (It was the custom of the Ishmaelites to wear gold earrings.)

²⁵ They answered, "We'll be glad to give them." So they spread out a garment, and each of them threw a ring from his plunder onto it. ²⁶ The weight of the gold rings he asked for came to seventeen hundred shekels, not counting the ornaments, the pendants and the purple garments worn by the kings of Midian or the chains that were on their camels' necks. ²⁷ Gideon made the gold into an ephod, which he placed in Ophrah, his town. All Israel prostituted themselves by worshiping it there, and it became a snare to Gideon and his family.

*Judges 8:22-27*

# 25. STATUES AND MONUMENTS

Judges 8:22-27

Rulers set up monuments. As we walk the streets of great cities, we see history in stone. These statues and monuments can be set up to the glory of God, or of other gods or of people. Our cities don't glorify just one thing: they are neither Jerusalem nor Babylon, and their kings are neither Christ nor Nebuchadnezzar—nor Gideon.

Gideon's tale ends here so sadly. This weakest of warriors had been reassured by the Lord time and again before the battle to save God's people from their Midianite invaders. Finally, God's constant love and support had given Gideon the courage he needed to obey the Lord. With a mere 300 soldiers he became the one through whom God won a great victory (see Judges 6 – 8 for the full story).

Understandably the people sought to make Gideon king, but he refused their offer. With humble wisdom he saw that their true desire was to dethrone God. Gideon was offered powers, riches and status on a plate—and he refused them! He is formidably godly here. Yet then he throws it all away with a last request.

Gideon made a monument to his victory, to his glory, to himself. It became an object of false worship and a terrible snare to Gideon and his family, tempting them to a level of ambition that ultimately brought them down with in-fighting and murder (Judges 9—if you read this chapter you need to know that Jerub-Baal is another name for Gideon).

It's rare to find a monument that commemorates something purely good. For instance, in a park in Norwich, our nearest city, there is a statue of a local hero, Horatio Nelson. Nelson was a man of incredible charisma and vanity: a tenaciously faithful friend and a faithless husband. As a sailor, ship's captain and, later, admiral over the entire British fleet, he was as brave as he was shrewd. He died achieving his great victory at Trafalgar, which paved the way for a century of British dominance of the sea. This was a dominance that allowed fortunes to be made and cities enriched by shipping enslaved people made in God's image from Africa to the Americas.

History is not simple. We are made in the image of our holy God, who is infinitely good, kind, loving and just. But we have marred that image horribly. The statues and monuments of our cities, rightly considered, invite us to recognize both the glory and the depravity of humanity: our bravery and brutality, generosity and greed. When is it right to praise God for what we see, and when should we lament the wickedness of human power? If we see only the good or only the evil, we are probably not seeing with the eyes of faith. If we see hopelessness, we have lost the full wonder of redemption. Instead we must wonder at just how Christ will work redemption here. We should marvel that he can bring total justice and peace after centuries of strife.

Even when we cannot imagine how he'll do it, we can know that one day he surely will.

## FOR TODAY

Do some research on some of the historical statues, monuments or buildings you'll see today, trying to find both things to praise God for and things that you can lament over because they speak of the depth of humanity's evil. Praise God that he will right all wrong and judge all wickedness.

## FOR THE FAMILY

### Ask

• Who is your favorite character from history? Who do you think is the worst villain you know about? Have you seen any statues today and learned about a new hero or villain?

• How is Jesus like the heroes? What does he do or say that reflects their courage, honesty or perseverance? And how is he totally different from the villains?

### Make

Who do you know who would be worthy of a monument or statue? Maybe you could make one out of LEGO or papier-mâché, or draw one. What would you write on the plaque to rightly honor that person without making them sound perfect?

# Wild
# Country

*⁷ The angel of the* LORD *found Hagar near a spring in the desert; it was the spring that is beside the road to Shur. ⁸ And he said, "Hagar, slave of Sarai, where have you come from, and where are you going?"*

*"I'm running away from my mistress Sarai," she answered.*

*⁹ Then the angel of the* LORD *told her, "Go back to your mistress and submit to her." ¹⁰ The angel added, "I will increase your descendants so much that they will be too numerous to count."*

*¹¹ The angel of the* LORD *also said to her:*

> *"You are now pregnant*
>    *and you will give birth to a son.*
> *You shall name him Ishmael,*
>    *for the* LORD *has heard of your misery.*
> *¹² He will be a wild donkey of a man;*
>    *his hand will be against everyone*
>    *and everyone's hand against him,*
>  *and he will live in hostility*
>    *toward all his brothers."*

*¹³ She gave this name to the* LORD *who spoke to her: "You are the God who sees me," for she said, "I have now seen the One who sees me."*

*Genesis 16:7-13*

# 26. GOD SEES

### Genesis 16:7-13

The wild country can be beautiful, but it has an edge to it. In a parched desert or even a remote valley, we know that death does not lie far away. A fall, a leg broken or a backpack lost and we are left praying for rescue. It's in these places that it's easiest to imagine how Hagar felt in Genesis 16.

This passage is part of a miserable section of Abraham's story. God had promised that Abraham's offspring would be more numerous than the stars in the heavens or sand on the shore. Yet childless Abraham and Sarah struggled to believe God, and so they came up with a plan to use Sarah's maid, Hagar, as a kind of surrogate for God's promise. With a sad inevitability this sin spawned rebellious contempt in Hagar, cowardly avoidance in Abraham and harsh jealousy in Sarah. The result was Hagar fleeing in desperation.

We find her pregnant and homeless in the desert. She's near a spring—clinging to life in the middle of the wilderness. No doubt she was aware of the irony of the metaphor. Her life must have felt like her situation: both were a wilderness in which she was alone and unloved with no hope, no way back and nowhere to go. That was where the angel of the LORD saw her.

He saw her, and he came to find her in the wilderness—

the literal wilderness and the wilderness of her ruined dreams and famished hopes, of her anxiety, dread and sorrow. He came with guidance and a promise. In verse 13 Hagar reverently names the Lord as "You are the God who sees me." He sees you too. Jesus is the God who sees his people and comes to us. We so often feel invisible and unnoticed. Others may overlook us, but Christ never will.

The wilderness is dangerous, with a brutal beauty. It is also lonely. It is in the wilderness that we are left to confront our very selves. Perhaps that is why we are drawn to it and yet fearful of it. Here we see ourselves: our sorrow and our sin, and the wildernesses that we have created or inherited, have been left in or forced into. Here, too, we see the "wilderness" of life that lies between Christ's rescue of us on the cross and his return. He can feel far away. Yet we know he hasn't left us alone but has sent us his Holy Spirit (John 14:16-18). The same Spirit who stood by Jesus for his whole life now stands by us. We are not alone.

As we see ourselves, we realize that we need a God who sees us. When Jesus sees us, he also loves us. He sets his face toward us and comes for us. Christ came to die in the loneliest place. He came to speak to us words of blessing and comfort, just as he did to Hagar. One day he will return for us. He sees the wilderness where we wander, and he will come. He sees us.

## FOR TODAY
The wilderness is a good place to set out your troubles before the Lord. Pray out loud in lamentation over your hurts and confession over your sins. Open the Bible to Hagar's history or Abraham's story (Genesis 12 – 25), or read of Christ being tempted in the wilderness (Luke 4:1-13).

## FOR THE FAMILY
### Ask
- What is good about having time alone? How can we use some of the time we have alone to grow in our faith?
- Sometimes time alone can just be lonely and sad. How can this story help us then?

### Do
Build a heap of stones in a lonely place and talk about how God sees us whenever we are lost and lonely in the wilderness. Perhaps share stories of Jesus' love toward you and encourage one another with his faithfulness. Mark this as a spot where Jesus met you, just as the Lord met Hagar.

*⁴ Then the L*ORD *said to Moses, "I will rain down bread from heaven for you. The people are to go out each day and gather enough for that day. In this way I will test them and see whether they will follow my instructions. ⁵ On the sixth day they are to prepare what they bring in, and that is to be twice as much as they gather on the other days."*

*Exodus 16:4-5*

# 27. GOD PROVIDES

M oses led 603,550 men of fighting age out of slavery in Egypt (Numbers 1:45-46). Adding their wives and sisters, the children and the elderly, and the many non-Israelites who fled with them, there must have been several million people under Moses' care (Exodus 12:37-38). Several million throats needing water and bellies needing food in the wilderness of Sinai.

I once visited Egypt. Driving through the wilderness, I saw the terrain God had appointed for this journey of faith. The dusty, stunted shrubs and blown, tired landscape made it abundantly clear that there would be little chance of anyone foraging enough to live on. To feed a mighty people would be impossible.

So God, who had saved them from Egypt, saved them again as they traveled to the promised land. He sent them bread from heaven: sweet, satisfying life for them day after day. The gift was also a test, though—a diagnostic to show the state of their hearts. They were told to only gather enough for each day, since the bread would come again in the morning.

This made sense. There would be no possibility of collecting, storing and transporting enough bread to give them security for their long journey. Their only chance was that God would continue to provide, day by day.

Their only chance lay in the trustworthiness of the God who had saved them from slavery and now rained down bread. To trust the God who had proven himself utterly faithful was the obvious thing to do.

Of course, some did not trust him and kept spare bread for the next day (Exodus 16:19-20). When they came to eat it, it was full of worms. We sometimes act in a similar way. Jesus took our death and judgment on the cross; he led us out of slavery to sin. He rose and gave us his life to live. He guides us through the wilderness and is himself the bread of life (John 6:35). And yet, day by day, I try to satisfy myself with worm-infested rot. I kid myself that I can live in the wilderness without Jesus—scavenging the peace, joy, hope and love that I need from my job, money or "likes."

Or I rely on yesterday's walk with Christ. I delight to worship Jesus with brothers and sisters on Sunday, built up by the love of my church family. Sometimes I then try to live through the week on that one meal—but day by day I stink more pungently. We need Jesus today. We cannot live now on yesterday's sustenance. Jesus is our *daily* bread (Luke 11:1-4). We must go to him daily.

Hiking with carefully allotted rations is as close as most of us get to "daily bread." The wonderful reminder of such times is that God provides for us. On our own we may have well-stocked freezers, but spiritually speaking we have only empty jars. Yet Christ is our portion day by day, in unfailing provision. Jesus himself is the bread that gives us life.

## FOR TODAY

If you are heading out into the wilderness, take your rations, snacks or picnic as an opportunity to remember how we need to come to Christ often, just as we need to eat often. You can't hike all day just on breakfast: you need regular sustenance. God gives us meals, highlighting our recurrent need for food, as a reminder of our more desperate, more frequent and more recurrent need of himself. Use each meal as a chance to pray and meditate on his blessings.

## FOR THE FAMILY

### Ask

- If you went for a long hike without any food, what would it be like?
- Trying to love God and love each other without listening to God in the Bible or talking to him in prayer is just as hard as hiking when you are hungry. Can you think of a way to help yourself pray regularly throughout the day today, just as you will have regular snacks?

### Make

Make a mess! Out of sight, scatter candy or chocolates on the floor or table (maybe wrapped ones!) just before you head out. Tell the children to look for manna from heaven as you arrive back!

*10 On the evening of the fourteenth day of the month, while camped at Gilgal on the plains of Jericho, the Israelites celebrated the Passover. 11 The day after the Passover, that very day, they ate some of the produce of the land: unleavened bread and roasted grain. 12 The manna stopped the day after they ate this food from the land; there was no longer any manna for the Israelites, but that year they ate the produce of Canaan.*

*Joshua 5:10-12*

# 28. GOD BRINGS US HOME

Joshua 5:10-12

Moses had led the people of Israel out of slavery in Egypt. They had grumbled against God, tested his love, stretched his patience and wandered from him. Yet the Lord stayed faithful to them. He did not cast them off or send them back to Egypt as they foolishly demanded. This is good news for us because we too are in the wilderness. Freed from slavery to sin and death by the suffering of Christ, we too are journeying to the promised land. We long for that day when Jesus will come again, when we will finally be home. The day when Jesus will lift his nail-scarred hand and wipe away the last tears from our cheeks.

As we wait for that glorious day, though—as we tramp on through this wilderness—we are so prone to complaining. We are often found whining, moaning and demanding that God pander to our desires as though we were gods and he our servant. It is such good news that God forgives us again and again. As we wander away and realize that the howling of the wolves is getting closer, we feel the arms of the Shepherd hoisting us onto his shoulder. He forgives and even runs after the sinner in the wilderness (Luke 15:4).

It is delightful to be led through the wilderness by our good Lord. Perhaps you are experiencing some wilderness delight yourself as you read this. It is delightful to be away from it all for a bit. It is also delightful, though, to come home. After a long walk—especially one where the weather closed in and you have fought wind or sleet—it is a relief to stagger inside and close the door. You shut it firmly against the gale and sigh with relief as you feel the warmth of the fire and hear the greetings of friends.

That is the sense of our passage. The journey had been long, endured over decades. The people had been sustained by the bread of God, and led by the hand of God, but now they were home. Finally camped in the promised land, they shared the Passover meal—the meal God had commanded as their way to remember that he had set them free (Exodus 12:21-28). They celebrated how God had kept his promises to them. The next day they ate from the abundance of this fruitful land, a land flowing with milk and honey: their home.

We too will be brought home. Our journey will not end in the wilderness; it will end in the promised land, the new creation. We might face terrible foes and impossible challenges, but our God and Guide is more than equal to them (Psalm 23:4-6). Jesus will lead us safely home, and, on that day when he returns, he will bid us to sit down and eat. He himself will feast us with the great meal of which every Passover, every Lord's Supper, every piece of manna and every gift of love is only a foretaste. We will eat in the promised land; we will be with Jesus, our Passover Lamb (Revelation 5:6; 19:9; 21:1-5); we will be brought home at last.

## FOR TODAY

Pay attention to your homecoming today. Do something relatively strenuous with your day so that your legs are tired, your feet sore and your stomach groaning. Then see just how good the coffee and biscuits, cold drink and chips, or stew and dumplings taste! Put your feet up to the fire, with a full belly and a glass at your side, and savor a hint of what it will be like when Jesus brings you home.

## FOR THE FAMILY

### Ask

- What is it like to come home after a long hike?
- What do you think it will be like when Jesus brings us to our forever home?

### Spot

Look out for hikers, cyclists and others who are on long journeys. You could make it a game, with points (one for a hiker or cyclist; an extra one for a pack or basket; another if they look really tired), or look out for the heaviest laden, most tired-looking or most relaxed (at a café)—or whatever you feel like.

# Leaving

¹ *Praise the* LORD.

*Praise God in his sanctuary;*
  *praise him in his mighty heavens.*
² *Praise him for his acts of power;*
  *praise him for his surpassing greatness.*
³ *Praise him with the sounding of the trumpet,*
  *praise him with the harp and lyre,*
⁴ *praise him with timbrel and dancing,*
  *praise him with the strings and pipe,*
⁵ *praise him with the clash of cymbals,*
  *praise him with resounding cymbals.*

⁶ *Let everything that has breath praise the* LORD.

*Praise the* LORD.

*Psalm 150*

# 29. ENDING WITH PRAISE

Psalm 150

In the first devotion in this book, Psalm 121 helped us consider the hopes and fears we brought away with us. We leave, too, with hopes and fears over our return to normal life. Heading back home, back to work, back to routine, back to the old rhythms and back to neighbors, church and chores usually brings mixed feelings. Joys and hopes have been rekindled, but there are also sorrows you are now bracing yourself to re-enter—alongside more mundane thoughts about where to pick up some essentials on the way home.

Wonderfully, we can once again take all these to God and place them in his hands, where it is safe for us to leave them. We can do so knowing that our lives, like the psalms, move toward unbridled praise. There is a progression in the book of Psalms—although, as with life, it is not a smooth one. When we reach Psalm 150, it's clear what everything has been heading toward. This psalm has only one command: to praise God. It gives us only very general reasons (in verse 2) because we have had 149 psalms to fill in the many specific reasons along the way. Psalm 150 is a song of unbroken praise!

Our lives, too, are heading toward such praise. As we see God more clearly, our hearts are increasingly filled with his praise. I have been blessed with good friends, some of whom have known me for decades. My appreciation for them and my understanding of their kindness and care for me have grown over the years. The same is true of God. As we see him more clearly in his word, as we experience his fatherly care of us in the suffering of life, and as we are overawed by the extent of his forgiveness of us, made possible by his Son, we turn more quickly, more naturally, and more completely to praise. As our knowledge of God grows, so does our praise—because to know God is to praise him.

Our destiny is to praise God face to face. Whatever your homecoming holds, it is not your final return. Our homes in this world are simply wayside inns on our journey to our true home with God. We will praise him when we get there. Yet, as those loved by Jesus, we can also praise him as we travel—whether through joys or sorrows. This is the hope with which we travel home. Why settle for turning our break into an Instagram story or leaving a five-star review on TripAdvisor when the true source of all we've enjoyed is God and we have the opportunity to praise him?

Where there are reasons for praise in the good time we have had or the good things we return to, let's be loud in our praise! Where these reasons are lacking—if our time away was another disappointment or we are braced for the difficulties of returning home—we can still be loud. Let's praise the Lord for his love, his presence, his kindness and his mercy toward us. Let's praise the Lord for neither avoiding the cross nor leaving us in the grave. Let's praise the Lord because he will give us the strength, grace and perseverance we need to complete our journey home to him. Let everything that has breath praise the Lord!

## FOR TODAY

Consider how you can set your heart on praising God. Think through the blessings you have in him and the kindness that he has shown you during your trip, and back home. Turn these blessings into a time of praise, perhaps using Psalm 150 and adding in your own verses in the middle, listening to or singing some praise songs. If you are away with your family, you could sing the children's favorite, or put some on in the car as you head out for the day.

## FOR THE FAMILY

### Ask

- What has been good about our time away, which we can praise God for?
- As we return home, what other gifts from God are there that we can praise him for?

### Do

As you load the car or pack your bags, use it as an opportunity to praise God. Each time you bring out a bag or put something in your suitcase, praise him— either for something related to the item or for something else that's praiseworthy about him.

*¹ Then I saw "a new heaven and a new earth," for the first heaven and the first earth had passed away, and there was no longer any sea. ² I saw the Holy City, the new Jerusalem, coming down out of heaven from God, prepared as a bride beautifully dressed for her husband. ³ And I heard a loud voice from the throne saying, "Look! God's dwelling place is now among the people, and he will dwell with them. They will be his people, and God himself will be with them and be their God. ⁴ He will wipe every tear from their eyes. There will be no more death or mourning or crying or pain, for the old order of things has passed away."*

*Revelation 21:1-4*

# 30. ANOTHER BRIGHT SHADOW

Revelation 21:1-4

All that was good about the last days or weeks was merely a flicker of the joy and peace we will know when Jesus comes. All that went wrong will be undone as we see his face. Neither Babylon, Boston nor Barcelona is an eternal city, but the heavenly Jerusalem is. In her is all the beauty and glory of creation, because in her is our Lord.

At best, the time you have had away from home will have been mixed. Hopefully joy and rest will have been the dominant notes, but they might not have been. Even if they were, as you leave they may well start to feel fleeting and elusive. I usually return home thinking I am a new man. My old, anxious self is gone, no longer to feel the darkness of winter or pressure of work. The new, tanned, rested me will surely never head down the miserable rabbit-hole of fretful worry again. Life is a summer's breeze!

Sadly, I am always wrong. No cabin in the woods or villa by the sea can cure me of my sin. When I return home, I will bring myself back with me. Yet one day that will not be the case. When I arrive at my eternal home, I will leave my old self behind as I rise from the dead. I will be transformed into my resurrection body in the twinkling of an eye (1 Corinthians 15:50-53). One day I will be in a new home that will be more magical and marvelous than any earthly destination. One day I will be with Jesus, and I will never have to leave (Revelation 21:1-4; John 14:2).

As you travel back, you may well be praising God. You will probably also be steeling yourself for the return. There are many things in our world that trouble us— even make us weep. Sometimes we do that quietly and secretly. There are fears and sufferings that we do not know how to share or who to share them with. Sometimes the tears flow freely. We are overwhelmed by the sorrow. This can be cathartic, but sometimes it is more bitter, because we know that we will weep again and cannot see an end.

There will be an end, though. If you follow Jesus, he will bring you home. He will take your face in his hands. You will glimpse the nail-marks of his love for you as he gently wipes away your tears so that you can see his smile and know that you are welcome. We travel to Jesus, we travel with Jesus, and it is Jesus who brings us safely home.

The heavenly city, the new Jerusalem that comes to earth, is a picture of the uniting of heaven and earth. There will be no separation. God will dwell with us. That is where we are heading. That is our home. Like a wakeful captain with a shipload of bruised and battered orphans, Jesus has his eyes on the harbor. Despite being lashed by the wind and rain, his hands are steady on the tiller as he pilots us safely through storms and rocks. He will bring us home. This trip, and this return, is meant to be a bright shadow of that greater trip and final homecoming. May it be so to you, and may it lift your eyes to the Jesus who is your God and your destiny.

## FOR TODAY

Sometimes there is too much to hold in our minds. As we leave and return, we will be full of thoughts, grateful for joys and aware of half-felt worries. It might be a day to listen to a song you love or to turn to a favorite Bible passage. Once you have listened or read, try to share everything that's in your heart with your kind Lord and good Father.

## FOR THE FAMILY

### Ask

- What are you looking forward to about going home? Let's thank God for these things.
- What makes you feel sad about leaving and traveling home? How can we ask God to help us with these things?

### Spot

As you begin your journey, spot places you enjoyed going to over the last few days. As you get nearer to home, spot places that are familiar and that you missed while you were away. You could make it into a "first to spot" game—if you have the energy left!